Developing Portfolios for Learning and Assessment

This book is a practical, accessible guide to implementing portfolio use for assessment and learning purposes. It focuses specifically on portfolio use in educational contexts and moves beyond description and general principles to analyse and discuss the impact of portfolio use on assessment, curriculum and pedagogy.

The author has extensive experience of using and researching the use of portfolios in a variety of teaching and learning settings. Throughout the book, practical examples are used to integrate theory and practice, and possible tensions and necessary supports are identified to assist the successful implementation of a portfolio system.

The book is essential reading for lecturers, teachers, teacher educators and students implementing portfolio use for learning, assessment and appraisal purposes.

Val Klenowski is a Senior Lecturer in Curriculum Studies at the Institute of Education, University of London.

Developing Portfolios for Learning and Assessment

Processes and Principles

Val Klenowski

London and New York

First published 2002 by RoutledgeFalmer
11 New Fetter Lane, London EC4P 4EE

Simultaneously published in the USA and Canada
by RoutledgeFalmer
29 West 35th Street, New York, NY 10001

RoutledgeFalmer is an imprint of the Taylor & Francis Group

Typeset in Goudy by Keystroke, Jacaranda Lodge, Wolverhampton
Printed and bound in Great Britain by The Cromwell Press, Trowbridge, Wiltshire

British Library Cataloguing in Publication Data
A catalogue record for this book is available from the British Library

Library of Congress Cataloging in Publication Data
Klenowski, Val, 1952–
   Developing portfolios for leaning and assessment : processes and principles /
Val Klenowski.
      p. cm.
   Includes bibliographical references and index.
   ISBN 0–7507–0988–X — ISBN 0–7507–0987–1 (pbk.)
   1. Portfolios in education.   2. Educational tests and measurements—
Great Britain.   I. Title.
   LB1029.P67 K58 2002
   371.26—dc21
      2001048585

ISBN 0–750–70987–1 (pbk)
ISBN 0–750–70988–x (hbk)

For Maria

Contents

Figures

Acknowledgements

I am grateful to the Education Department of Western Australia for granting me permission to use extracts from the First Steps and Stepping Out Literacy Programmes, the Student Outcome Statements 1997 Sample Book and the Guidelines for Preparing a Teaching Portfolio. I also appreciate and wish to acknowledge the agreement from the Scottish Qualifications Authority for permission to use extracts from the Scottish Examination Board Certificate of Sixth Year Studies English Guidance for Teachers on the Creative Writing Folio and the Kentucky Department of Education for permission to use the Kentucky Writing Assessment (Holisitc Scoring Guide) from Kentucky Department of Education KIRIS Writing Portfolio Assessment Grade 4 Assessment Training Book. The Curriculum and Qualifications Authority in England have also kindly granted permission for the use of the 1995 Specifications for the Intermediate Business Organisations and Employment Unit 1. I also wish to acknowledge the permission granted by Taylor & Francis Ltd, 11 New Fetter Lane, London, EC4P 4EE to use material published previously in an article 'Portfolios: promoting teaching', that appeared in *Assessment in Education*, 7, 2 (2000), pp. 215–36.

Many colleagues and friends have contributed to my understanding of the subject presented in this book and it is difficult to select a few. There are many others who have helped in the production and offered me support during the writing when times were difficult. I wish to give particular thanks to Janet Harland for her helpful comments, suggestions and encouragement throughout; to Christine DeLuca for explaining the use of folios in the Scottish education system; to Ros Ashby for sharing with me the professional portfolio for the Post Graduate Certificate in Education History Course; to my colleagues from Hong Kong, Kevin Blachford for the encouragement he gave at the outset, to Jenny Chan researcher on the project, Sharon Bryant, Andy Timmins, Li Pak Hung, colleagues and pre-service teachers at the Hong Kong Institute of Education; to colleagues at the Institution of Education in the Curriculum Studies and Assessment Guidance and Effective Learning groups, particulary Denis Lawton, Pat Tunstall, Caroline Lodge and Gordon Stobart for their helpful advice. Other colleagues, friends and my brother George have offered kind support and encouragement that has been special.

Finally I would like to acknowledge RoutledgeFalmer and wish to give particular thanks to Anna Clarkson for seeing the potential and understanding the circumstances throughout the writing of this book.

Introduction

Aims of this book

The use of portfolios for learning and assessment is becoming internationally popular. Artists, writers, photographers, advertising agents, models, architects and the like have traditionally made use of portfolios to present work samples and examples of their best or distinctive work. Today portfolios are found in all phases of education and professional development for learning, assessment, promotion and appraisal. A portfolio of work can be used for development and assessment of subject knowledge, acquisition of teaching skills and reflective practice, professional and vocational preparation and employment.

This book has several aims. The first of these is to provide professionals, educators and students with guidance on how portfolios have been used for assessment and learning purposes and to illustrate their potential. The contexts of teacher and medical education, primary and secondary classrooms have been included to explain the processes and principles involved when using portfolios. The technical and management issues that have emerged in these contexts are described. Case-study material is used to illustrate the range of factors that need to be considered when planning to use portfolios.

The second aim is to analyse and discuss the impact of portfolio use on assessment, curriculum and pedagogy. Key issues, major tensions, constraints and the necessary supports for developing and implementing a portfolio system are identified. The interrelationship of portfolio assessment to curriculum and pedagogy and required changes to teaching and learning are described. Research evidence gathered from the use of portfolios in teacher and medical education and practical examples from primary and secondary classrooms are incorporated to explain the range of purposes. For example, the move to an outcomes-based curriculum in Australia has resulted in states, like Western Australia, using portfolios for developmental assessment purposes in primary schools while in Scotland portfolios are used for summative assessment at secondary level.

The third aim of this book is to analyse relevant learning theories that underpin this form of assessment. Practical examples are used throughout to describe and analyse the integration of learning and assessment theories with practice. The tensions that exist when using portfolios for learning *and* assessment purposes, at the same time, are emphasised to indicate how unintended outcomes can emerge and to highlight the possible problems and pitfalls. Examples are given to help describe these issues in detail.

Why portfolios?

There are many theoretical and practical reasons why portfolios are being used in a range of contexts for a variety of purposes. There has been dissatisfaction with assessment approaches derived from a quantitative tradition. For example, recently in England there have been numerous claims that 'students are becoming over-examined' (Hackett, 2001), that we are 'testing our children to destruction' (Guttenplan, 2001) and that it is time 'to trust teachers' (Henry, 2001).

More qualitative, expansionist approaches such as the portfolio provide an alternative. Portfolio use for assessment aligns with current assessment and learning theory. Insights into the alignment of assessment, curriculum and pedagogy through the use of portfolios are discussed throughout the book. It is argued that portfolio use for assessment and learning offers the opportunity to redress the imbalance caused by testing and mechanistic and technicist conceptualisations of curriculum and assessment.

The use of portfolios for a range of purposes has the potential to make more explicit the important relationship between curriculum, assessment and pedagogy. This is because the use of portfolios for assessment helps provide a structure and processes for documenting and reflecting on teaching and related learning practices, and making them public. While much emphasis has been given to the emergence of a new assessment paradigm (Gipps, 1998a; Assessment Reform Group, 1999) the theoretical relationship between curriculum and assessment remains under-represented. Recently, there has been acknowledgement of the need to develop theoretical unity such that the reformed visions of curriculum and assessment for learning align with pedagogy. Shepard (2000) and Looney (2000) have emphasised the need to build a symbiosis between curriculum and assessment policy that is reflected in pedagogical practice. The use of the portfolio offers the opportunity for the realisation of this important integration of assessment with curriculum development and is a theme addressed throughout.

Educators aspire to develop reflective students or professional teachers; research findings conclude that the use of portfolios promotes the development of important skills such as reflection, self-evaluation and critical analysis. Portfolios are being used increasingly for assessment and learning purposes because of the potential for the associated curriculum and pedagogic practices to foster metacognitive development. Tools for metacognition and their connection to the skills needed for learning and understanding need to be understood. These important skills are outlined and their integration into the portfolio process is discussed in chapter 2.

What is a portfolio?

In 1992, Arter and Spandel indicated that the term portfolio had become a popular buzz word; however, they stressed that it was not always clear what was meant or implied by the term, particularly when used in the context of portfolio assessment. These authors offered the following definition:

> . . . a purposeful collection of student work that tells the story of the student's efforts, progress, or achievement in (a) given area(s). This collection must include student participation in selection of portfolio content; the guidelines for selection; the criteria for judging merit; and evidence of student self-reflection.
>
> (Arter and Spandel, 1992: 36)

This definition acknowledges the developmental nature of the assessment process involved and emphasises the importance of the active involvement of the students in portraying what they know and can do. Another significant dimension to this definition is the recognition of the purpose of student reflection on the learning processes involved in the work accomplished and the integration of assessment with teaching and learning. The definition of a portfolio is developed further throughout the book but for now what is important to emphasise is the centrality of student self-evaluation and reflection and the opportunity to portray the processes by which the work in the portfolio is achieved.

Torrance (2000) has described how assessment practices need to develop to identify:

> *what* pupils think is a reasonable answer in a particular context, but also *why* they think this – what are their criteria for response, and what do they think of the teacher/examiner's assumptions? Assessment should also be concerned to find out *what else* it is that pupils know, and *want* to know, since this will form the core of a genuine dialogue about the purposes, processes and desirable outcomes of schooling; the core, in fact, of a high(er) quality educational experience, leading to higher educational standards.
>
> (Ibid., 186)

He suggests that such an approach to assessment would acknowledge that 'some pupils may be in a state between knowing and not knowing – learning, in fact, and being able to continue to learn' (ibid.).

A portfolio of work that incorporates self-reflection supports learning if the developmental nature of the portfolio process is sustained and provides opportunities for students to self-evaluate their own growth. Students need the cognitive tools to be able to understand their development. This is why metacognition is an essential process that needs to remain central to the development of a portfolio of work and is an important aspiration for alternative forms of assessment such as the use of a portfolio.

How are portfolios used?

The use of the portfolio is an educative process in itself. This is because the development of the portfolio of work to be assessed and the submission of this work is a phase in ongoing learning. The portfolio of work remains a factor in activity. The evidence in the form of the product of the portfolio is a demonstration of learning but at the same time requires the student to develop important insights, skills, strategies, dispositions and understandings for continuing learning.

The metacognitive growth that is intended in the development of a portfolio of work suggests that it is a means by which students may demonstrate their learning but more importantly involves processes and a mode of learning that encourages them to take responsibility for their own continuing learning. The concept of 'freeing of activity' (Dewey, 1916) has been influential in the way in which portfolio use for assessment and learning purposes has been conceived in the writing of this book.

The portfolio is not in itself the end. The associated assessment and pedagogical practices and processes help develop successful learning. Learning occurs, as a consequence of these processes, beyond the submission of a portfolio of work. There is continuous, ongoing development that aligns with Dewey's (1916) notion of aims as continual and ongoing human activities. In describing the criteria of good aims Dewey indicates that the term 'end in view' is suggestive of termination or conclusion of some process. 'Strictly speaking, not the target but *hitting* the target is the end in view' (ibid.: 123). Dewey did not accept the separation of ends from means. This is true for the use of portfolios. It is not the product in isolation but both process and product that are important. Current assessment systems that support educational aims by focusing rigidly on targets to the detriment of student and teacher agency – choice of means and processes of action – *have got it wrong*.

Dewey in describing the concept of 'freeing activity' emphasises that the end or object is not the end in itself, it is the doing with the thing or end that is important. For example, the portfolio of work is not the only intended outcome; 'it is a factor in activity' (Dewey, 1916: 123). A portfolio of work could be a record of one's development to be used for improvement purposes or it could be that it is used to demonstrate one's best work in order to attain a qualification, promotion or new position. 'The doing with the thing, not the thing in isolation, is [the] end. The object is but a phase of the active end – continuing the activity successfully' (ibid.). The development of a portfolio of work requires important cognitive and metacognitive skills such as monitoring, planning, reflecting and self-evaluation. In this way the portfolio cannot be separated from the processes involved in its development. This is what Dewey means by 'freeing activity'.

In this book the principles and processes involved in the development of a portfolio are emphasised. The belief is that separation of ends from means is educationally unsound. For students of today there is a need to continue learning beyond school and to develop means that will enable them to achieve success, fully and freely, through the realisation of their self-initiated ends. The aim or end is in Dewey's terms 'a means of action'. Creativity, curiosity, conversation and critique are some of the means of action of the portfolio process.

There are still limitations, problems and constraints associated with this approach. However, the processes involved in the development of a portfolio engage students such that they focus on their own learning strategies and achievements. The progress and the quality of their learning are valued over how much has been learnt and whether the knowledge represented in the portfolio matches a centrally predetermined objective response.

The portfolio includes more that one indicator of achievement. There are several entries that reflect a range of assessment types; for example, essay answers, research projects, video-recordings of presentations or exhibitions of learning. There can be ample opportunities for the promotion of individual learning and thinking skills. Students are active in their learning, and the development of their skills can occur in authentic contexts.

The assessment of the portfolio is designed formatively so that there are more opportunities for students to receive feedback. Developmental assessment is integrated into the process and a criterion reference system is used. The teacher assumes the important role of facilitator of learning and is engaged actively in the assessment task. The professional judgement of the teacher is respected and he or she is expected to work collaboratively in the development of progress maps or learning continua that require the analysis of performance. Such assessment practices enable a wider range of knowledge, skills and attitudes to be recorded. This learning is enabling. Students gain valuable skills in organisation, evaluation, reflective thinking and management. Skills such as these allow the students to continue learning and thus to improve their employability in times of uncertainty and continual change.

What can you use a portfolio for?

Internationally, the contexts and purposes for portfolio use are expanding. The many reasons why educators advocate the use of portfolios for assessment purposes in education and professional development are developed more fully in chapter 1. The portfolio is used for assessment, appraisal and promotion in the field of education. In teacher education, for example, portfolios are used for assessing the achievement of pre-service teachers and serving teachers, and in medical education they are learner-centred focusing on the individual's identified professional development needs. Lecturers in higher education and serving teachers are expected to present portfolios for promotion and appraisal. Students in primary and secondary schools develop portfolios of work for assessment and exhibition purposes. In the vocational education field portfolios are used extensively for the assessment of competencies.

Structure and content of the book

The first chapter explores the various purposes of portfolio use. These purposes include summative assessment, certification, selection, appraisal, teaching and learning. For each use an illustration from a particular learning and teaching environment is given to portray the associated processes involved. The portfolio in terms of product is outlined and the relevance of evidence in the assessment process is highlighted. Specific examples of learning outcomes and suggested samples of evidence are given to illustrate how a portfolio is developed and how the evidence selected is used to demonstrate the attainment of standards.

Portfolio processes are evident in the various phases of producing and collecting the work, selecting work for illustration of competence and reflection on the various forms of evidence to understand and demonstrate development and achievement in learning. Self-evaluation, reflective practice, collaboration and conversation are fundamental processes considered in the next chapter. Much research has been conducted in teacher education and for this reason the development of reflective practice through portfolios is explored in this context.

Portfolios and related assessment concepts form the themes of chapter 3. The changing emphases in assessment are outlined at the beginning of this chapter. The use of criteria is discussed first; competence, achievement and criterion-referencing follow. The important role of formative assessment in the portfolio process is emphasised. Feedback and its integral role in assessment and learning is described in detail. Aspects of validity (construct, consequential and predictive) and issues related to validity and learning are introduced. The assessment of the portfolio raises the importance of understanding the standards and issues related to reliability. Summative and holistic assessment of the portfolio are attended to at the conclusion of the chapter. Examples of grade descriptors are given and the holistic use of criteria in summative assessment is outlined. Important research findings that relate to the holistic assessment of portfolios for summative purposes are shared.

There are many aspects to consider when implementing a new form of assessment such as portfolios. The weaknesses, problems and pitfalls are analysed fully as a cautionary measure. The procedures and support needed for implementation are described in contexts such as initial teacher education or vocational education programmes. The implications are identified for a range of teaching and learning settings. The strengths of the portfolio process are also presented to provide a balanced perspective to the constraints that are summarised in chapter 4.

The fifth chapter is a case study of an attempt to use portfolios for assessment and learning purposes in an initial teacher education course. It is included to share with readers the developmental process in the implementation of a portfolio and the implications for pedagogy and learning. It provides insights on the procedures, practices and resources involved. Important lessons from the experience are described and the implications expanded for others to consider in their own attempts to set up and implement portfolio systems for assessment.

The sixth chapter deals with the principles and processes that underpin the use of portfolios for learning and assessment purposes. The six principles that underpin the use of portfolios are derived from research conducted by this author. Each principle is discussed and highlighted using illustrations from research and a review of the literature. The first principle deals with the focus on learning. The types of learning and learning styles supported through portfolio use are described. The impacts on cognitive and affective development are analysed. The second principle focuses on the developmental process. Issues related to growth, and development in scope, are explained. The documentation of achievements, of analyses of teaching and learning experiences and inclusion of process artefacts is the third principle. The inclusion of process artefacts is a unique feature of the portfolio. Self-evaluation is integral to portfolio use and this fourth principle is emphasised. The fifth principle relates to the processes involved in the collection, identification and selection of evidence and reflection on the work in the portfolio. Finally the role of the teacher as facilitator is the sixth principle included in the discussion. Portfolios are being increasingly used for professional preparation and appraisal purposes. For promotional purposes teachers, lecturers and administrators are being asked to present a portfolio of evidence. The role of the portfolio in career advancement to demonstrate professional knowledge and as a strategy to improve one's effectiveness as a lecturer, teacher or administrator is discussed and illustrated. The implications for educators and policy-makers conclude this chapter.

Chapter 7 examines the concept of a portfolio in relation to important theories of learning, curriculum and assessment. The conceptual framework that underpins the change to using a portfolio for assessment and learning purposes is described to illustrate the important relationship between the learner, learning and assessment. Theories of learning presented by Dewey (1916), Vygotsky (1978) and Bruner (1990) are drawn upon and the implications for pedagogy are described. The driving forces behind the change in current assessment practices derive from the context of globalisation and information technology. These forces are described to explain why and how assessment practices for the future are changing. Reference is made to the corresponding changes needed in the curriculum for the twenty-first century.

Tensions

There are many tensions associated with the use of portfolios for assessment and learning purposes. The first relates to these purposes. Is it possible to use a portfolio as a vehicle of assessment and for purposes of facilitating learning, researching practice and/or professional development?

The second tension relates to the current context of a market economy. Education systems, internationally, have been driven by accountability pressures and/or standards that have to be met at all levels. For example, in England and Wales, the Office for Standards in Education (Ofsted) performs ongoing inspections at primary, secondary and tertiary levels. In addition, the Teacher Training Agency (TTA) has developed bureaucratic standards for use in teacher education. There exist requirements at national (National Qualified Teacher Standards), institutional, subject and individual levels. These policies have resulted in an over-regulated system that creates a context that is not conducive to innovative processes and developmental approaches to assessment, as embodied in the portfolio. In such contexts of accountability, numerical indicators are more seductive to politicians, political advisors and parents. The creation of league tables, for example, has enabled politicians to identify so-called successful and failing schools and in theory has helped parents in their choice of school. Is it possible to use the portfolio as a mode of appraisal and assessment in a highly regulated system at the same time as using it as a means of validating one's personal development as a professional? For example, an initial teacher in England is confronted with the major dilemma of addressing the TTA standards while somehow trying to maintain a sense of self and personal identity as a teacher. Can teachers address these standards and still maintain their own identity in such a regulated system? The vision of a teacher is complex and demanding. Can a portfolio capture fully the complexities of teaching? These questions are addressed as much of the work, on the use of portfolios for assessment and learning purposes, has been exemplified in teacher education.

At the outset, it is beneficial to acknowledge the inexorable existence of pressures to pervert. In a context that is standards-driven, and values standardisation, there is a great danger that technical, rationalist approaches, that generalise and make superficial the portfolio process, will emerge. In generalising about the portfolio process there is also the real possibility that processes could be trivialised. The problems and pitfalls of portfolio implementation are included to demonstrate how and when some of these issues emerge and specific cases are used to demonstrate how some of these issues have been addressed.

Using the portfolio to support learning and teaching practice, and to empower learners, is difficult in a context that favours traditional methods of raising standards by assignments, exams and observations. In England and Wales, the National Record of Achievement was to be a planning tool and a record of achievements. Broadfoot (1998a: 466) in analysing why Records of Achievement (RoA) did not survive, states that the 'emancipatory discourse associated with RoA initiatives translated into categoric discourse of recording achievement in the context of the development of National Assessment'. It is conceivable that using portfolios primarily for summative assessment and accountability purposes could follow the same fate. When assessment is introduced for comparability purposes, and national requirements are stipulated, what can happen is that tasks are simplified. For instance, when the task is generalised and reduced to a generic level, it is no longer as demanding. This is because the serious, specific nature of the task is lost. By way of illustration, the intended processes of critical self-evaluation and reflection integral to the development of certain portfolios could give way to unintended outcomes such as using checklists to ensure that the requirements of a standardised structure are met, thereby reducing the assessment to superficial and trivial purposes.

Another tension that is relevant particularly to the prevailing policy context of England is that the use of portfolios for assessment and learning is neither an easy nor inexpensive option. To implement a portfolio assessment system requires time and considerable funds for teacher and resource development. There is much work required not only on the part of the teacher in terms of change in curriculum, pedagogy and assessment practices but also on behalf of the student. Developing a portfolio of work for summative assessment purposes, for example, requires time and effort for conceptual thinking and metacognitive development. In a climate where quick results in terms of quantifiable outcomes are valued, an expansionist assessment system that values processes *and* products will experience numerous tensions and constraints.

The portfolio is in its infancy and has the power and potential to transform. However, in the promotion of the portfolio for assessment and learning purposes there is the possibility that too much will be promised and in practice a lot less will be accomplished. Yet it is vital that alternative methods are explored fully in the search for improved methods for learning and assessment that empower students to learn, help them manage that learning and develop vital skills for success in the twenty-first century.

1 Using portfolios for a range of purposes

Assessment purposes

> Different kinds of portfolios result from, and are appropriate for, different educational contexts and purposes. A portfolio that serves the assessment needs of a classroom teacher, for example, may not be the most appropriate form of portfolio for use in a state assessment program. There is no one 'portfolio'; there are many portfolios.
>
> (Forster and Masters, 1996: 1)

Portfolios can be used for learning, assessment, appraisal and promotional purposes, and the contexts for portfolio use continue to develop and expand. In teacher education, for example, portfolios are being used increasingly for assessing the achievement not only of pre-service teachers but also serving teachers. Lecturers in higher education and serving teachers are expected to present portfolios for promotion and appraisal. This chapter will explore how portfolios are used for a range of assessment purposes in a variety of contexts including primary, secondary and vocational settings.

Assessment fulfils a range of aims. Black (1998) distinguishes between formative, summative and accountability purposes, while Torrance and Pryor (1998) expand on each of these functions to include the promotion of learning through the use of helpful feedback, certification and selection and the accountability of schools through the publication and comparison of results.

The fundamental issues in assessment design are, firstly, 'fit for purpose' and, secondly, the need for the mode of assessment to impact positively on teaching and learning (Gipps, 1994). When using portfolios for assessment purposes both these principles of design apply. The essential consideration in the assessment design of the portfolio is the evidence selected for inclusion. As Forster and Masters (1996: 2) indicate, all portfolios are 'sources of evidence for judgements of . . . achievement in a range of contexts, from classroom monitoring of student performance to high-stakes summative assessment. All . . . contain "pieces of evidence". The more relevant the evidence, the more useful it is for inferring a student's level of achievement in a learning area.'

A portfolio of work can fulfil the full range of various assessment purposes: accountability, summative assessment, certification, selection, promotion, appraisal and formative assessment in support of teaching and learning processes. Each particular purpose requires varying processes for the collection and selection of evidence. These processes include critical self-evaluation, reflection, meta-cognition and substantive conversation. Descriptions of the various purposes are now offered while the processes integral to the creation of a valid portfolio of work are discussed in the following chapter.

Portfolio use for summative purposes

For summative or certification purposes, the portfolio is usually considered along with other evidence. In situations requiring high-stakes decisions the portfolio is embedded within a more comprehensive learning and assessment system. For example, in England, Wales and Northern Ireland in the implementation of a portfolio system of assessment for the General National Vocational Qualifications (GNVQs), government officials and ministers insisted that the system had to be credible for selection purposes. As Wolf (1998: 422) points out, in the 'United Kingdom credibility effectively means external examinations'. The GNVQ assessment system has consequently undergone continuous change since it was introduced but does still require the student to produce a portfolio of work. Recent changes have shifted the emphasis to tests and external assessments, reducing the benefits of using the portfolio for learning and assessment purposes. This will be discussed more fully in chapter 4.

The use of portfolios in the Scottish education system is discussed next in relation to summative purposes, and is an example of high-stakes assessment embedded within a more comprehensive learning and assessment system. The Scottish system is described in proportionately more detail than the other sections in this chapter because the use of portfolios for summative purposes also relates to the purposes of selection and certification. Different examples and contexts have been used to illustrate these latter purposes and to demonstrate the range of contexts in which portfolios have been employed. However, to emphasise the detailed level of specification needed when using portfolios for assessment purposes that are considered high stakes, a full description of the Scottish system is offered first. Such systems need to be comprehensive and the many technical and resource considerations necessary are described.

Assessment for summative purposes is designed to provide quality information about a student's performance without impacting negatively on good teaching and learning practice. For administrative reasons such assessment is usually time-efficient, manageable and inexpensive. An adequate level of reliability is needed for comparability purposes. A consistent approach and consistent grading must be implemented to ensure equity and fairness. Moreover, consistency of standards ensures quality in the overall assessment process and outcomes (Gipps, 1994). Using portfolios for summative purposes requires the specification of standards and contents by education authorities for formal assessment and monitoring.

In the Scottish education system students are expected to produce portfolios (called folios[1]) of work in certain subjects. It is in the subject areas of English, art and design, drama, and the creative aspects of technological and computing studies that the folio of work is relevant. Within the Scottish system 98 per cent of secondary students, aged fourteen to sixteen years, study at Standard Grade (equivalent to the General Certificate of Secondary Education (GCSE) in England and Wales). This involves two years of study (Years 10 and 11) at Credit Level (assessing grades two and one), General Level (assessing grades four and three) or Foundation Level (assessing grades six and five), generally in seven or eight subject areas. Assessment of these subjects typically requires one-third of the course to be internally assessed. The overall forms of assessment used include examinations, performance-based projects, investigations and folios.

Higher Grade in Scotland is broadly equivalent to the first year of A Level study in England and Wales. Students are sixteen to seventeen years old. Forty-one per cent of the age group gains an award in at least one Higher Grade subject in Year 12. Typically students choose up to five subjects. In Year 13 a minority of those staying on (12 per cent of the age group) pursue their studies at Certificate of Sixth Year Studies (CSYS), equivalent to Upper Sixth. Few would take more than two subjects at this level. The Scottish sixth year is also used to broaden the students' curriculum at Higher Grade.

First, the extent to which standards and folio contents are specified by the Scottish Qualifications Authority (SQA) (which incorporates the former Scottish Examination Board) for formal assessment and monitoring purposes will be illustrated. This will be done by reference to the summary of arrangements for the subject of English at Standard Grade level (Scottish Examination Board, 1996). The course consists of four modes: reading, writing, listening and talking. The interdependent nature of these modes is recognised, and for the purpose of certification the listening mode is subsumed under talking. This results in the three assessable elements of reading, writing and talking. The latter element is internally assessed and does not have implications for the folio. Reading and writing are externally assessed and require the development of a folio of coursework and separate written examinations.

The instructions given to teachers regarding the folio of coursework in the subject of English at Standard Grade are as follows.

> For each candidate, a folio of work containing *five* pieces of extended writing . . . will require to be submitted to the Board . . . for assessment. The pieces in the folio should comprise the candidate's best work and should be selected by the candidate in consultation with the teacher from work undertaken throughout the course. Two grades will be awarded for the folio, one for Reading and one for Writing.
>
> (Scottish Examination Board, 1996: 1)

The Board provides full details of the course and assessment arrangements, including statements of the grade-related criteria, specimen question papers and guidance for candidates and teachers on the production and submission of the folio.

The current Higher Grade course in the subject English follows on and extends the activities pursued at Standard Grade. The study of language through literature pervades the course, and the assessment system allows freedom of choice of the literary texts that will best encourage development and enrichment. The examination consists of: a personal studies folio, worth sixty-five marks; and two papers: Paper I (two hours, five minutes), worth seventy-five marks, and Paper II (one hour, thirty-five minutes), worth fifty-five marks. The personal studies folio is submitted to the SQA for assessment and contains two pieces of coursework in reading and writing undertaken during the year of presentation. These include a review of personal reading (RPR) and either a piece of imaginative writing or a piece of discursive writing. The review of personal reading is an extended piece of writing (1,000 to 1,500 words in length) based on a detailed independent study of a single literary text, or set of short texts, or a comparison of two or more texts, which has (have) not been taught. Excessive length is penalised. Reviews which exceed 1,800 words in length incur a penalty of up to 25 per cent of the available marks. The text(s) are selected by the candidate in consultation with the teacher and are the subject of personal study by the candidate. The review itself is also the work of the candidate. Candidates cannot use the text(s) central to the review of personal reading in answering any other part of the examination, other than in the situation which might arise where an unseen passage set in Paper II, Part 1, Section A (Practical Criticism) coincides with the candidate's choice.

The candidate, in consultation with the teacher, chooses the topics for imaginative and discursive writing. In the case of the imaginative writing, the written piece takes one of the following forms; its length should be appropriate to the form chosen:

- an essay reflecting on personal experience;
- a piece of prose fiction (short story; episode from novel);
- a poem or set of thematically linked poems;
- a dramatic script (e.g. scene, monologue, sketch).

Candidates opting for the discursive writing are required to produce an extended piece of continuous prose of approximately 600 to 800 words in length. Excessive length is penalised. Discursive writing pieces that exceed 960 words in length incur a penalty of up to 25 per cent of the available marks.

Candidates are informed that in generating items for inclusion in the personal studies folio, they should be advised of the dangers arising from plagiarism and/or collusion with others and of the significance of the candidate declaration that accompanies the submission.

The Scottish Examination Board (predecessor today to SQA) has produced guidance for candidates studying English at Higher Grade relating to the personal studies folio. To further illustrate the degree of specification given by the Scottish Examination Board for the folio of work, reference is made to the various documents provided. These include:

- the summary of arrangements for Higher Grade English (Scottish Examination Board, 1996);
- the Higher Grade English Personal Studies Folio Guidance for Candidates (Scottish Examination Board, 1994a);
- the Higher Grade English Personal Studies Folio Guidance for Teachers (Scottish Examination Board, 1994b); and
- the Guidance for Teachers on Assessment Part 1, The Personal Studies Folio (Scottish Examination Board, 1991).

This latter document deals with the assessment of the personal studies folio: the review of personal reading, imaginative writing and discursive writing.

These documents inform both teachers and students about the contents and the fact that the folio is worth a third of the marks in Higher Grade English. Students are told that they are expected to complete two pieces of written work: a review of personal reading based on texts they have chosen and a piece of imaginative or discursive writing. The length of each piece is given, the penalty incurred if the length is exceeded in all instances is outlined, as are the possible marks that could be attained for each piece. Students are also informed about how to choose what to write, and how to organise their writing, in the review of personal reading. They are made aware of what the examiners will be looking for in grading their reviews. Similar information is given regarding the imaginative and discursive writing. Candidates are urged to present their written work in a legible manner, to indicate the sources or secondary material they have consulted and to state the number of words used in the review of personal reading and in the discursive writing. Candidates must sign a statement to indicate that the work is their own and their teacher must also sign a statement to this effect. The document concludes: '*If your teacher cannot sign the statement, the Folio is not submitted to the Board*' (Scottish Examinations Board, 1994a: 2). Authenticity in this respect is an important component of reliability.

Teachers of Higher Grade English are also given guidance about the personal studies folio. At the outset it is stated that the personal studies folio 'has provided candidates with the opportunity to produce extended, well-organised pieces of writing' (Scottish Examination Board, 1994b: 1). The document offers clarification on the length of the RPR and discursive writing, the subject matter and the production of the work to be included in the personal studies folio. An exemplar of good practice is given:

- Teachers are expected to brief all candidates on the nature of the task (which includes the issuing of *Guidance for Candidates*), and to offer practical suggestions as to how best they might choose their subject areas.
- Deadlines for submission of work should be established.
- Teachers are informed that they should encourage candidates to consult with them on a regular basis in order to establish how the task is developing and offer guidance that will allow each candidate to develop his or her thinking on the chosen topic. It is suggested that the teacher should, for example, ask

questions, and candidates should be encouraged to seek reasons for their responses to the text(s).

- Teachers are also encouraged to look closely at a first draft, but are informed that they should make it clear that they are not there principally to correct errors, to supply ideas or to take responsibility for production.
- Teachers are also expected to ensure, as fully as they can, that the work finally submitted is the candidate's own, so that the teacher can sign the declaration. '*If you cannot sign the declaration, the Folio should not be submitted to the Board*' (Scottish Examination Board, 1994b: 2).

Teachers are informed of their legitimate role in the production of the Personal Studies Folio, by offering guidance and support as necessary. It is stressed that a vital aspect of this role is to ensure that all candidates are aware of the dangers of plagiarism and collusion with others and of the significance of the candidate's declaration that accompanies submissions.

In addition to the above information teachers are offered guidance in the context of an assessment procedure which is carried out by the Board's examiners and is wholly external to presenting centres. It is considered beneficial for teachers to have information on standards of performance aligned with appropriate mark ranges when preparing and presenting candidates for the examination and in drawing up their estimates of candidate performance. Thus the guidance given includes introductory statements on the Folio and the Report, the relevant marking instructions for each component of the examination, and graded exemplars of performance. For each exemplar a commentary is offered, referring to the marking instructions and explaining briefly how the mark was assigned. It is stressed that what is important to note is not just the final mark but the process by which the mark was determined. Teachers are encouraged to make candidates aware of the marking instructions since these may be helpful in providing them with targets for their writing.

To illustrate the degree of specificity given to teachers as guidance in their teaching and formative assessment roles of the creative writing folio the requirements, assessment and category descriptions will be outlined. The guidance that will be used for explanation purposes here is concerned with the reflective essay and forms part one of a guidance pack on the creative writing folio at Certificate of Sixth Year Studies. There is equivalent type and amount of guidance given for parts two, three and four that are focused on poetry, drama and fiction respectively. At the outset it is emphasised that the creative writing folio is a folio of imaginative writing and that the reflective essay is an imaginative writing form. The main requirements set out that the reflective essay will:

- aim to give pleasure, not, as a rule, information;
- concern itself with, usually, a single idea, insight, experience; (or where more than one idea, insight or experience is involved, the treatment of these by the writer will give unity);
- be genuinely contemplative; its tone may be confidential, amused, concerned or even indignant;

- communicate to the reader a clear sense of the writer's personality;
- not merely offer the product of reflection but engage the reader in the *process* of reflection.

It is stated that in the last analysis this process of reflection is the distinctive quality of the reflective essay. These basic features are what examiners look for in their assessment of the legitimacy of items submitted by candidates in the category of the reflective essay. Teachers and candidates are told that they might find it helpful to check that these features are present in any piece of writing to be submitted as an example of the reflective essay. At Higher Grade, the reflective essay is an essay reflecting on personal experience, but at CSYS the reflective essay is not so strictly limited to matters reflecting on personal experience and can be on:

- a person, place, an object;
- a condition, situation, relationship;
- a mood, memory, feeling;
- an image, idea, insight;
- an issue, activity, theory.

In choosing a topic and in preparing for reflective writing, candidates are told that they should consider carefully:

- the extent to which they themselves have gained personal insight(s) from their contemplation of the topic;
- the appropriateness of the stance and tone they intend to adopt in their treatment of the topic (as this will determine the entire structure of the essay);
- the extent to which their intended treatment of the topic will allow the reader to share their personal insights.

The statement is made that, while it is possible to recognise these features and to acknowledge the range of legitimate topics, it is not possible to be prescriptive about the form of the reflective essay and therefore aspects of possible treatment are given. Only two examples are given here for illustration purposes:

- the impression of a mind exploring an idea: moving around it or moving it around or holding it up as if to a light for inspection;
- the suggestion of an apparently random treatment, in the course of which insight is gained as if by accident.

Whatever form the essay takes candidates are informed that the effect should be:

- to reveal to the reader the distinctive, individual voice of the writer;
- to convince the reader of the appropriateness of the stance and structure adopted;
- to produce in the reader aesthetic satisfaction, the hallmark of the reflective essay and, indeed, the hallmark of all forms of effective creative writing.

Figure 1.1 Assessment criteria for all forms of creative writing in the creative writing folio

Theme/content
To what extent is there, at the heart of the piece, a recognisable theme/point/insight?

Structure/form
To what extent does the piece have a structure appropriate to the task it sets itself?
To what extent are the conventions of the chosen form (reflective essay, fiction, poetry, drama) recognised and respected?

Stance/tone/mood
To what extent does the writer adopt a clear stance in relation to the reader and/or to the material he or she is working with?
To what extent does this stance produce in the piece an appropriate and sustained tone or mood?

Expression/style
To what extent does the writer demonstrate skill and competence in use of language appropriate to CSYS?
To what extent is the style of writing appropriate to the chosen form?

Source: Scottish Examination Board (1992).

Certain exclusions, such as writing that is transactional or discursive in effect, are given to further indicate what is required.

The guidelines for the assessment of the reflective essay stipulate that the markers must be satisfied that the piece of writing is legitimate as a submission in the category of the reflective essay against the above requirements. The criteria for assessment are then given (see Figure 1.1) and these apply to all forms of creative writing in the folio.

The piece of writing is then placed according to the balance of its qualities at an appropriate point in one of the five categories (see Figure 1.2 for category 1). The final assessment is expressed as a numerical mark on a fifteen-point scale. The category descriptions are outlined for five categories and the marks allocated for the attainment of a category are given. For example, category 1 is for fifteen to thirteen marks, category 2 is for twelve to ten marks and so on until category 5 is described and is for three to one marks. A mark of zero is reserved for work that is not a legitimate form of imaginative writing under which it is submitted and unacceptably slight or trivial. When the zero mark is given, markers must refer the script to the examiner. To illustrate the descriptive detail of each category, only category 1 will be given here.

In this example of the use of portfolios for summative purposes the emphasis is on manageability and reliability of evidence. Consistency of approach is highlighted by the provision of guidance to students and teachers. The consistency of standards is attended to by the provision of exemplars, marking instructions and commentary for each exemplar to indicate how the mark was assigned. In the

Figure 1.2 Category 1 description and mark allocation

Category 1 (15–13 marks)
Theme/content
There will be an impressive degree of insight/perception/imagination. The reader will feel that, at the heart of the piece, something original/exciting/surprising has been captured/created/communicated.

Structure/form
Although it may be unobtrusive and even, on occasions, quite subtle, the structure of the piece will be totally appropriate to the writer's purpose and, in its overall shape, aesthetically pleasing. The conventions of the chosen form will have been recognised, its constraints respected and its potential exploited with an impressive degree of resourcefulness, skill and imagination.

Stance/tone/mood
The stance adopted by the writer in relation to the reader and to the material that has been shaped and presented will be clear and appropriate. The reader will be constantly aware of the writer's distinctive voice. The tone will be skilfully controlled and sustained. An appropriate mood or atmosphere will have been effectively created.

Expression/style
The writing will be controlled, vivid, original, fluent – exploiting the possibilities of language with resourcefulness and subtlety to achieve desired effects.

Source: Scottish Examination Board (1992).

provision of advice there is comprehensive detail given on a range of exemplar essays and examiner's commentaries on each. The detail of the examiner's commentary on each exemplar essay includes an analysis of how, and the extent to which, the writing meets the main preliminary requirements of the reflective essay and how the assessment criteria are addressed.

Portfolio use for certification and selection purposes

Portfolios are also used for the assessment purpose of certification and selection. It is in the context of teacher education where this application of portfolio use is most prevalent. The certification and selection function of assessment provides the student with a statement of achievement for entry to a profession or for entry to higher education. It is detailed to provide comprehensive coverage of attainment and is reasonably reliable to ensure confidence in the results and comparability across institutions. The focus is on the technical aspects of assessment for credential and selection purposes. The use of portfolios for these purposes requires the contents, or types of evidence for inclusion, to be specified by an awarding body or education authority. An example of the use of portfolios for such purposes will now be described by reference to the teacher education context.

In the United States the use of portfolios in teacher education has accelerated at both the local and national levels. For example, at the local professional level portfolios are used in teacher education programmes in the education of new teachers. At the national level the National Board for Professional Teaching Standards (NBPTS) has incorporated the use of portfolios for Board certification of experienced teachers (Lyons, 1998a).

The establishment of standards for high levels of competence in the teaching profession in the United States and in England and Wales has highlighted the importance of:

- professionalism;[2]
- teachers' lifelong learning;
- teachers' knowledge;[3]
- ethical and moral stance;
- knowledge of students and their learning difficulties;
- teaching theories and strategies;
- knowledge of teaching resources; and
- subject-specific teaching knowledge.

These standards reflect the complexity and demands for achievement of teacher status. This is why educators, such as Shulman, have developed assessments that accommodate and capture the multifaceted nature of teaching and the performance of effective teachers. Standards and performance assessments that focus purely on outcomes without clarifying the conception of teaching and learning they incorporate, are not helpful (Lyons, 1998b).

The portfolio, for certification or selection purposes, is usually developed from an externally defined set of standards. It generally consists of a collection of work that is representative of the individual's strengths and portrays the student in the most favourable light. From the outset it is important to consider the warning from Snyder *et al.* (1998: 123–4). They advise that proving one's competence on state or nationally defined teaching standards can dominate over portfolio use as an opportunity for a teacher to record growth through critical reflection on the tensions and failures common to the learning process. They rightly question whether the use of a portfolio for summative assessment overrides its use as a strategy and process to make visible one's own practice for the purpose of reflection and inquiry.

In teacher education, for high-stakes purposes such as certification or selection, the use of a portfolio is usually considered with other evidence such as classroom observations and assessments of collaborating teachers. Shulman, quoted in Lyons (1998b: 15), asserts 'that the process–product, input–output model of teaching that dominated assessment failed to capture the complex, messy, multiple dimensions of teaching and of teacher learning'. Shulman stresses the need for the assessment of teachers to include 'both content and process'.

The Extended Teacher Education Programme (ETEP) at the University of Southern Maine is a fifth-year innovative, professional development school model teacher education programme, designed for liberal arts graduates, that leads to teacher certification after a one-year placement. At the outset of the programme pre-service teachers are informed of a set of goals or standards that are used for certification. They are also informed of the ETEP outcomes that are described under the following eleven areas:

- knowledge of child/adolescent development and principles of learning;
- knowledge of subject matter and inquiry;
- instructional planning;
- instructional strategies and technology;
- assessment;
- diversity;
- beliefs about teaching and learning;
- citizenship;
- collaboration and professionalism;
- professional development;
- classroom management.

Construction of a portfolio is a requirement. It consists of evidence indicative of competence, such as a statement of one's teaching philosophy, classroom lessons, student work in written and video formats. Critical conversations interrogating one's practice and carried on with mentors and peers over the course of the programme is expected in the development of a portfolio. Such conversations inspire further reflection on the contents of the portfolio. These thoughts are documented and relate to why particular entries are selected for inclusion, the entries themselves, what the teacher has learned from the experience of teaching and learning, why this is important, and the meaning of their own learning. A portfolio presentation to university and classroom faculty and peers then takes place. Finally a decision about certification is made on the basis of the portfolio and other work of the pre-service teacher (Lyons, 1998b; Davis and Honan, 1998).

For certification purposes the portfolio is considered with other evidence such as classroom observations and assessments of collaborating teachers. The portfolio of work provides evidence indicative of competence.

Portfolio use for appraisal or promotional purposes

Portfolios used for appraisal or promotional purposes include evidence to support the professional development or promotional aspirations of the individual. The employer provides explicit criteria for selection or appraisal and the individual is responsible for selecting portfolio evidence that demonstrates his or her competence in relation to the criteria.

The nature and focus of the structure of the portfolio vary. The focus of the portfolio is selective and, in a teaching context, highlights the core professional and pedagogical knowledge or competencies of the individual teacher. The evidence is collected over time and is representative of both student and teacher work. Some reflective commentary or evaluative statement is included to explain the selected evidence to others, such as appraiser or employer.

The Education Department of Western Australia has produced guidance for teachers aspiring to the position of Advanced Skills Teacher (AST). The guide lists the competencies that need to be addressed and the types of evidence that could be used to illustrate competence. Figure 1.3 illustrates one of these competencies and indicators of attainment.

Further guidance on how to compile a teaching portfolio has been published by various professional organisations and committees. For example, in Australia the

Figure 1.3 Level 3 classroom teacher competencies and indicators of attainment

Competency 1

Utilise innovative and/or exemplary teaching strategies and techniques in order to more effectively meet the learning needs of individual students, groups and/or classes of students.

Indicators of attainment
- A rationale for the introduction or use of a particular innovative strategy/technique is developed.
- Innovative/exemplary teaching strategies/techniques are developed to more effectively meet the learning needs of individual students, groups and/or classes of students.
- Innovative/exemplary teaching strategies/techniques utilised assist students to 'learn how to learn'.
- Innovative/exemplary teaching stategies/techniques are implemented within a supportive learning environment: an environment in which there is recognition and respect for difference and diversity; and sensitivity to matters of gender, cultural difference, social class, disability, family circumstance and individual difference.
- Teaching strategies/techniques are developed and implemented in response to school and system level initiatives.

Source: Education Department of Western Australia (1997a).

Federation of Australian University Staff Associations (FAUSA) has produced a guide. It describes the portfolio as a summary of an academic's major accomplishments and strengths in the area of teaching. It provides a list of what an academic might select to include. The stress is on choosing evidence to illustrate teaching competence and to give a favourable impression. Four categories of material for inclusion are given. The first category is factual information or hard data, such as courses or numbers of students. Second is selected factual material to portray the image of a good teacher. The third category is uncorroborated claims such as descriptions of teaching innovations or reading journals. The final category relates to the opinions of others, such as student feedback or letters of praise.

Information detailing how the teaching portfolio should be structured is given. Teachers are advised to select from a given list of items that might be relevant to the teaching accomplishments of an Australian academic. The list comprises items organised into the following areas:

- introduction;
- information about courses and supervision;

- description of current teaching practices;
- student achievement;
- scholarship in teaching (i.e. evidence of interest in and of steps taken to evaluate and improve it);
- evidence of student reactions to teaching;
- other evidence of reputation as a teacher (Roe, 1987).

It is stressed that this is only a suggested list and that additional items can be included to reflect the individual's unique approach to teaching.

Portfolio use to support learning and teaching

Assessment, to support the learning and teaching, aims to help students develop and further their learning. Such assessment is enabling rather than limiting and in this context the role of assessment is formative. The particular student's learning needs and the development of his or her motivation and confidence are paramount. Formative assessment is therefore dominant and requires a high level of validity while the same degree of reliability is not as important for this purpose of assessment. Portfolios used for this purpose include content selected by the student, by the teacher, in collaboration of teacher and student, in collaboration with peers or in collaboration between mentor and student.

In England in Higher Education (HE), Burke and Rainbow (1998) have described the use of portfolios for the documentation of key-skill development. They have found that portfolios can help students improve their self-assessment skills, provide evidence for tutor evaluations and for potential employers. 'Improving own learning and performance' is seen as the overarching key skill that provides the framework within which other skills such as communication, application of number, information technology, problem-solving and working with others can be refined.

Burke and Rainbow (1998) state that the problem in HE is how to monitor student progress in each skill, over time, in different modules, assimilating the separate assessments of a range of tutors and lecturers. They maintain that a portfolio can provide the focus for review, reflection, target-setting and action-planning by the student. Evidence of progress and achievement is collected in the portfolio which, when properly managed, can help raise overall achievement.

In this context the student manages and compiles the evidence for the portfolio. Work that reveals significant evidence of learning and/or key skill competence is selected based on student–tutor agreement that this chosen work meets the given criteria. The work reflects evidence of:

- progress over time;
- understanding of a key principle or process;
- lack of understanding and hence of future learning needs;
- originality and creativity;
- achievement in different contexts and
- key-skill development.

Annotation of selected evidence, so that it is clear to the tutor why and when the evidence was selected, is a further requirement for the development of this key skill portfolio. In this HE context the portfolio is updated regularly so that evidence demonstrates:

- a higher level of achievement;
- improved understanding; and
- that a previous weakness has been overcome.

Types of evidence selected to demonstrate key-skill competence vary and are derived from different sorts of written and visual work (such as essays, minutes, diaries, reports, questionnaires, photographs, plans, models, film/video, graphs, maps, etc.). Observation evidence that is noted by a tutor or mentor authenticating that the student achieved something significant can be included. Evidence from extra-curricular activities, such as work experience, is also acceptable.

Burke and Rainbow (1998) emphasise that the greater the variety of evidence and the better its quality the more it will confirm that the student has demonstrated the key skills in a variety of contexts on different occasions. The evolving picture of the student's development is captured in the portfolio and can be used as the focus for regular review between tutor and student or to enable the student to self-evaluate for improvement of learning. These authors outline the review process that is set against a previous action plan. The following questions direct the review:

- What skills, concepts and knowledge have been demonstrated?
- Is there evidence of progress over time?
- Is there any significance about the contexts from which evidence was drawn?
- To what extent has the previous action plan been met?
- What should be the next targets for the student, either in terms of remedial work or progressing to new work?

The main responsibility for managing the portfolio rests with the student.

Portfolio use for professional development purposes

The portfolio used for professional development purposes in a teaching and learning context includes materials and samples of work that provide evidence for critical examination of teaching and learning practices. Teachers reflect on and evaluate their own teaching practices; they are also able to engage in dialogue with others which helps to highlight the complexity and diversity of those teaching and learning practices.

Shulman (1998) suggests that portfolios may be important as a professional development activity through peer review. He was the first to suggest the value of a teaching portfolio in providing an opportunity to discuss one's teaching (Shulman, 1992). Others have since recognised the importance of sustained conversations about teaching and learning with colleagues in refining the portfolio. It is for this reason that Davis and Honan (1998) use teams to support the portfolio development process because mentors and peers provide support, give feedback, listen actively, ask questions and offer different perspectives thereby strengthening the portfolio development process. They conclude that the structure and associated portfolio-based conversations help foster reflection about teaching and enable pre-service teachers to better articulate their beliefs about teaching and learning.

The development of the portfolio is a collaborative process. This involves mentored or coached teaching practice and substantive conversations about the teaching and learning. Grant and Huebner (1998: 159) indicate that the portfolio should include 'a reflective commentary, the result of deliberation and conversation with colleagues, which allows others to examine the thinking and pedagogical decisions behind the documented teaching'. They refer to the work of Shulman and acknowledge 'that teacher constructed portfolios make teaching public, including making explicit tacit knowledge, in order to increase professional autonomy, and making public the standards and good work as a source of future wise action'. Shulman (1998: 34) maintains that research becomes part of the educational community's discourse; however, teaching has remained a private act. His argument for peer review and portfolios in teaching is that 'they contribute to making teaching community property in colleges and universities and, therefore, put teaching and research into the same orbit'.

Grant and Huebner (1998: 152) recommend that portfolios for teachers in a professional development context should be:

- designed to promote reflective practice;
- shared with colleagues;
- encouraged for cooperating and student teachers;
- a bottom-up voluntary process that is owned by teachers and not used for evaluation purposes; and
- supported by enabling conditions.

They stress that 'key benefits are lost if the reflective culture of professional development is replaced by a culture of compliance where teachers go through the motions of assembling materials according to a predated checklist'. Grant and Huebner (1998) emphasise two key purposes of portfolio development. First, to develop the habit of mind that views teaching as inquiry; second, the habit of mind that views collaborative learning as the way to come to know teaching.

Cuban (1998) describes a post-tenure review portfolio experience as a collaborative venture and indicates that what was so different with the portfolio experience from the usual tenure review was the clear focus on improving, rather than judging, and concentrating on issues raised by himself and others as they met. The shortcomings of the process related to the lack of structure to the discussions and the uncertainty he faced about what a portfolio, which was focusing on a review of teaching and research, should contain.

Portfolios for professional development allow teachers to consider the complex, multifaceted nature of teaching by providing the opportunity to reflect critically on their practice, to engage in professional dialogue with colleagues and to collaborate and develop understanding and ideas on teaching and learning. It will be argued in the next chapter that these processes are integral to the development of any portfolio. Self-evaluation, substantive conversation and reflective thinking and practice need to be incorporated into the portfolio development phases and have important implications for the pedagogic practices adopted.

Summary

- There are many portfolios used for a range of purposes: learning, teaching, assessment, appraisal, promotion and professional development.
- The range of assessment purposes for which a portfolio can be used include: accountability, summative assessment, certification, selection, promotion, appraisal and formative assessment in support of teaching and learning processes.
- All portfolios contain 'pieces of evidence' and the more relevant the evidence the more useful it is for evaluating the level of achievement.

2 Key processes in portfolio development

For the purposes of this book, which considers the use of portfolios in a wide range of contexts, pupil learning through to teacher professional development, the following definition of a portfolio has been developed.

A portfolio is a collection of work that can include a diverse record of an individual's achievements, such as results from authentic tasks, performance assessments, conventional tests or work samples. A portfolio documents achievements over an extended period of time. Generally, the individual identifies work from an accumulated collection to illustrate achievement and to demonstrate learning for a particular purpose, such as certification, summative or formative assessment. Careful, critical self-evaluation is an integral process and involves judging the quality of one's performance and the learning strategies involved. The individual's understanding of what constitutes quality in a particular context and the learning processes involved is facilitated by discussion and reflection with peers, teachers, lecturers or tutors during interview, substantive conversation, exhibition or presentation of learning. The development of the portfolio involves documentation of achievements, self-evaluations, process artefacts and analyses of learning experiences, strategies and dispositions. It is significantly more than a collection of assignments.

Learning processes

The above definition is generated and adapted from research and work completed over the past five years by the author. It emphasises the key processes that have been identified as important in the development of the portfolio. It also acknowledges the student's central role in learning and assessment.

A range of definitions of the portfolio has developed which illustrates the growth and diversity of portfolio use. These definitions incorporate features such as: criteria for the selection of pieces of work; assessment criteria; a time frame for the collection of work; and an indication of the extent to which individuals are involved in the selection and/or the assessment processes (Black, 1998; Crockett, 1998; Gardner and Edwards, 1998; Cole et al., 2000).

Shulman (1998: 37) defines a teaching portfolio as 'the structured, documentary history of a set of coached or mentored acts of teaching, substantiated by samples of student portfolios, and fully realized only through reflective writing, deliberation, and conversation'. The learning processes inherent in developing a portfolio are made clear in this definition. The way in which the development of the portfolio not only documents and records learning but also supports learning processes and strategies is emphasised. There is also the potential to support ongoing professional development through the portfolio development processes (Wildy and Wallace, 1997).

The previous chapter examined the portfolio according to the assessment purpose for which it was developed. Whether the portfolio is created for the purpose of summative assessment, certification, selection, appraisal or promotion, or whether it is developed to support teaching and learning or aid in professional development, there will be key processes involved. These processes include self-evaluation, substantive conversation and reflective thinking and practice. Metacognitive development is also included because the associated curriculum and pedagogic practices involved in the development of the portfolio can contribute to the development of metacognitive skills. These learning processes are discussed in detail as they are fundamental to the creation of a valid portfolio of work and central to the argument of this book that the product in the form of the portfolio of work cannot be separated from the essential processes integral to its development.

At the conclusion of the chapter the context of teacher education is used to illustrate these processes in practice as it is in this context where an exemplary use of portfolios to assess and support teaching and learning has become widespread.

Tenets

In the preceding discussion of various definitions of portfolios and the associated learning processes, several underlying tenets or principles emerge. The first relates to the purpose of the portfolio and how the identification of purpose together with the criteria and guidelines can assist the student in selecting work for inclusion.

Second, by involving students in the assessment process and by making clear to students that self-evaluation is important for demonstrating what has been learnt, and also how this has been achieved, an important message about what is valued in assessment is being communicated.

Third, the developmental nature of learning is promoted by the integration of assessment with the curriculum, teaching and learning. Students are required to focus on their own learning over time and have the opportunity to include samples of work from authentic learning tasks while at the same time reflecting on the strategies and processes used in such learning.

As suggested by these tenets, portfolios for assessment purposes represent a move from traditional forms towards more authentic forms of assessment. This shift is discussed more fully in chapter 7.

Self-evaluation

The development of a portfolio requires one to select from a collection of work to demonstrate competence achieved to a particular standard. Selecting work to demonstrate achievement requires students to think critically about their learning, to understand the standards of performance that drive their work and to critique their own work in relation to these standards.

It is helpful to make clear the distinction between criteria and standards. Sadler (1985: 285) defines criteria as the 'dimensions relevant to an evaluation' and standards as 'particular levels used as reference points'. This distinction is elaborated by Maxwell (1993: 293):

> the terms 'criteria' and 'standards' are not always distinguished, even in discussions of assessment, though it is useful to do so . . . Criteria are the various characteristics or dimensions on which the quality of student performance is judged. *Standards* are the levels of excellence or quality applying along a developmental scale for each criterion.

Consider the creative writing folio for Certificate of Sixth Year Studies of the Scottish education system described in chapter 1. Markers are informed that once each piece of writing is accepted as fulfilling the main requirements set out in the guidance for teachers then each piece will be assessed according to the assessment criteria that apply to all forms of creative writing in the folio. The criteria given are:

- theme/content;
- structure/form;
- stance/tone/mood;
- expression/style.

These criteria are expanded in the form of questions – as, for example, for theme/content: 'To what extent is there, at the heart of the piece, a recognisable theme/point/insight?'. Similarly the criteria are expanded for structure/form: 'To what extent does the piece have a structure appropriate to the task it sets itself? To what extent are the conventions of the chosen form (reflective essay, fiction, poetry, drama) recognized and respected?' (Scottish Examination Board, 1992: 6).

The piece of writing is then placed according to the balance of its qualities at an appropriate point in one of the following five categories. The final assessment is then expressed as a numerical mark on a fifteen-point scale. The developmental scale in this context includes the following category mark ranges:

- category 1 for which a candidate could attain 15–13 marks;
- category 2 for which a candidate could attain 12–10 marks;
- category 3 for which a candidate could attain 9–7 marks;
- category 4 for which a candidate could attain 6–5 marks;
- category 5 for which a candidate could attain 3–1 marks.

The standards for categories 1 to 5 are described in detail. To illustrate the level of detail, category 5 is given in Figure 2.1.

Figure 2.1 Category 5 description and mark allocation (SEB, 1992: 9)

Category 5 (3–1 marks)
Theme/content
Evidence of insight/perception/imagination will be difficult to discern. The reader will feel that there is no real heart to the piece, that little that is worthwhile has been captured/created/communicated.

Structure/form
There will be virtually no evidence of an attempt to shape and organise the material or, where a structure exists, it will be seriously flawed.
The conventions of the chosen form will largely have been ignored.

Stance/tone/mood
There will be little or no evidence of a serious attempt by the writer to adopt an appropriate stance or create an appropriate tone or mood.

Expression/style
The writing will, for the most part, be competent but there will be little or no evidence of the creative use of language to achieve desired effects.

Source: Scottish Exam Board (1992).

Sadler (1985: 286) states that 'criteria and standards constitute two of the key elements of evaluative discourse, [and] it is possible for reliable judgements to be made even when no criteria are used explicitly'. He adds that in such cases the evaluations are only valid to the extent that the evaluator is accepted as authoritative and competent. Sadler's notion of a hierarchical structure to organise criteria is useful to clarify further the importance of the student's role in self-evaluation of work for the portfolio. Sadler suggests that any given criterion can be expressed either as a component of some higher-level criterion or in terms of a number of lower-level criteria. Higher-level criteria have been described as axiological or 'zero-level' criteria. An example of this level of criteria for the creative writing folio discussed above would be 'theme/content'. They are in fact 'underlying values' or 'values proper.' Axiological criteria have to be decomposed for their substance to be known. That is, criteria are necessary in order for the content to be specified. For example the criteria of 'insight/perception/imagination' and 'something of worth has been captured/created/communicated' help to illustrate the substance of the axiological criteria of 'theme/content'. Sadler continues:

> axiological values develop only in the context of experiences, traditions, and evaluation that is from ground up. Although the label of an axiological value is compact and convenient, it applies to a rich and generalised idea whose power lies in its ability to transcend particular cases. In any concrete situation, a meaning appropriate to the context has to be generated.
>
> (Ibid.: 290)

Teachers and lecturers need to understand that higher-level criteria develop 'from the ground up' and that a meaning appropriate to the context has to be generated. Students also need to understand this concept if they are involved in self-evaluation. The implication is that teachers need to explain to students why the quality of an outcome or performance is better than another and this can best be done in relation to the context in which the notion of quality is developed. To illustrate this concept, a student who is assessed at category 5 for the creative piece included in the folio, described above, will need to be informed that they are not producing the quality of outcome which is valued. The student will need to understand what is meant by 'there is no real heart to the piece' and 'a degree of insight/perception/imagination that is not easy to discern' for the axiological criterion of theme/content. The teacher's role is to provide feedback on this work in relation to the category 4 criteria to help the student understand how learning can be taken forward. It is important that the feedback provides guidance that is manageable for the student given the particular category at which the work has been assessed. The use of exemplar essays can also assist in this process. It has been emphasised by Sadler (1989: 121) that:

> the indispensable conditions for improvement are that the student comes to hold a concept of quality roughly similar to that held by the teacher, is able to monitor continuously the quality of what is being produced *during the act of the production itself*, and has a repertoire of alternative moves or strategies from which to draw at any given point . . . students have to be able to judge the quality of what they are producing and be able to regulate what they are doing during the doing of it.

It is for these reasons that self-evaluation, substantive conversation and reflective thinking and practice are crucial to the development of a portfolio of work.

The selection of work for the portfolio requires the individual to self-evaluate, which is a learning process in itself. This is because when one evaluates, or judges 'the worth' of one's performance, strengths and weaknesses are identified for the purpose of improving one's learning outcomes. The self-evaluator identifies explicitly what it is that he or she finds meritorious and the criteria that are used. In a developmental context the other important factor is for the self-evaluator to identify the implications for future action. In this way the student monitors and judges aspects of his or her own learning.

Self-evaluation has been described in terms of developing students' ability to make judgements about the quality of material. When they identify areas for improvement in their learning they need to think about what action in terms of information or research that they need to find or complete. Improved learning in this context is linked to an understanding of criteria and what constitutes quality in a given context.

The term self-evaluation is used in a broader sense than self-assessment because it refers to ascribing value to the learning experience, first in the identification and understanding of the criteria and standards used, second by judging what is considered meritorious and third by synthesising the implications for future action. In a context of learning and teaching this is a developmental process that is supported and managed together with the teacher and the student's peers. This self-evaluative process is also broader than self-assessment as students are engaged in more than just ascribing grades or identifying the standard attained. They evaluate their performance and indicate progress against criteria and standards that emerge from the performance, have been given, are self-selected or negotiated with the teacher or peers.

The term self-evaluation emphasises that it is the students themselves who are conducting the evaluation. For such evaluation to be useful the outcomes should facilitate decision-making about action to be taken by the student. This concept of self-evaluation, then, parallels the notion of improving teaching and learning practices through teacher reflection on classroom practice (Stenhouse, 1975). The difference is that in self-evaluation it is the student who is engaged in reflection on his or her learning processes and teaching experiences.

Definitions of evaluation (Stake, 1979; Simons, 1987) emphasise the notion of 'ascribing value'. Wiggins (1989: 708) indicates that evaluation is most accurate and equitable when it entails human judgement and dialogue. He states that '[w]e rely on human judges in law and in athletics because complex judgements cannot be reduced to rules if they are to be truly equitable'. The implication here is that self-evaluations provide insights into a student's thoughts, understandings and explanations. Through the process of self-evaluation it is possible to better understand an individual's progress by checking out if selected evidence and the given rationale for selection meet the identified standard. This suggests that in order to explore the full potential of a portfolio of work, dialogue is needed at some stage in the evaluation process to ensure that the individual is fully examined.

Substantive conversation

The acts of constructing, presenting and reflecting on the contents or evidence of a portfolio are powerful portfolio processes for teachers and students at all stages of their teaching and learning.

For example, pre-service teachers collect work, make a selection and reflect on that selected piece of work that relates to their teaching or learning experiences. They may consider evidence such as lessons taught, evaluate samples of student work, analyse teaching experiences that have been successful and those that have not been so successful, and explain why these are important to their philosophy and practice. Lyons (1998a: 5) indicates that 'validation and understanding emerge through portfolio conversations with peers, mentors, the presentation of portfolio evidence, and recognition of the new knowledge of practice generated through this process'.

The importance of dialogue, interview or 'learning conversation' in the assessment process has been recognised (Broadfoot, 1986; Munby with Philips and Collinson, 1989; Francis, 1994; Smith, 1994). Owens and Soule (1971: 60) believe that:

involving pupils in an assessment dialogue is a simple means of providing a wealth of insight into the impact of teaching, how an individual pupil is coping with that teaching and its effects upon him [or her]. In particular, it can elicit information which must otherwise remain the exclusive property of the pupil, but which may be of vital importance to the teacher in relating to that pupil.

This follows the learning theory on which this book is based and Vygotsky's notion of the zone of proximal development. The dialogue that takes place is a form of focused intervention and enables joint problem-solving in the zone of proximal development with guidance from the teacher (or someone more skilled than the student).

Information gained from dialogue with the student is very relevant for the teacher when one considers Gipps's (1994: 4) contention that 'different forms of assessment encourage, via their effect on teaching, different styles of learning'. Formative and developmental forms of assessment are fundamental to the portfolio process and require dialogue between teacher and student. This interaction helps students identify strengths in their own learning and preferred learning styles. When this metacognitive insight of the student is shared with the teacher, it is valued as it assists the teacher in the facilitation of further learning.

Metacognitive development

Metacognitive development is an important aspiration for alternative forms of assessment such as the use of a portfolio. Metacognition involves thinking about one's own thinking or knowing about one's learning and oneself as a learner.[1] From exploring various definitions and empirical foundations of metacognition, Hacker (1998) concludes that: 'It is important that human beings understand themselves as agents of their own thinking. Our thinking . . . can be monitored and regulated deliberately, i.e., it is under the control of the thinking person' (Kluwe cited in Hacker, 1998: 10).

More recently metacognition has been defined as 'conscious and deliberate thoughts that have other thoughts as their object. As conscious and deliberate, metacognitive thoughts are not only potentially controllable by the person experiencing them, but are also potentially reportable and therefore accessible to the researcher [or teacher]' Hacker (1998: 8). This definition emphasises that metacognition is derived from an individual's own internal mental representations of his or her external reality. These metacognitive thoughts include what the individual knows about that internal representation, how it works and how the individual feels about it. For learning purposes it is important to know how, when, where and why one learns best as well as what constitutes acceptable standards in a range of contexts.

It is also important to be aware of one's own emotions in the learning situation. Claxton (1999: 41) indicates that: 'there is a strong need to understand the place of emotions in learning, and to develop the ability to contain, manage and tolerate them. This is one of the core ingredients of "emotional intelligence", and nowhere is it more crucial than in the domain of learning.' When an individual has this self-knowledge it is possible to be self-regulating and to take control by planning, monitoring, evaluating and implementing changes. This is important in the twenty-first century where individuals find themselves facing the unknown and in a context of constant change and unpredictability.

The various dimensions of metacognition include 'active monitoring', 'consequent regulation' and 'orchestration of cognitive processes' to achieve cognitive goals (Flavell cited in Hacker, 1998: 7). Metacognition requires interpretation of ongoing experience (Brown cited in Hacker, 1998) and can take the form of checking, planning, selecting and inferring (Brown and Campione in Hacker, 1998). Metacognition therefore involves the notion of making judgments about what one knows or does not know to accomplish a task (Flavell and Wellman cited in Hacker, 1998). Metacognition has been refined in meaning by being conceptualised in terms of metacognitive knowledge, which includes thinking about what one knows, metacognitive skill which refers to thinking about what one is doing, and metacognitive experience which includes reasoning about one's current cognitive or affective states (Hacker, 1998).

Today self-appraisal and self-management of cognition are considered to be fundamental characteristics of metacognition. The former refers to an individual's own thoughts about their knowledge and abilities, their affective states about their knowledge, abilities, motivation and characteristics as learners. The latter, self-management refers to thinking about thinking in action that helps an individual to organise aspects of problem-solving.

Hacker (1998: 11) concludes that definitions of metacognition need to include, 'knowledge of one's knowledge, processes and cognitive and affective states' and 'ability to consciously monitor and regulate one's knowledge, processes and cognitive and affective states'. Metacognitive knowledge has been described in terms of declarative, procedural and conditional knowledge because self-appraisal answers questions about *what* one knows, *how* one thinks, and *when* and *why* to apply certain knowledge or strategies (Paris, Lipson and Wixson cited in Paris and Winograd, 1990: 17).

Metacognitive research has occurred in the areas of cognitive monitoring and cognitive regulation (Nelson and Narens, 1994). An important finding, relevant to using portfolios for assessment, is the importance of accurate self-assessment of what is known for effective self-regulation. When students are aware of the state of their knowledge they can then effectively self-direct learning to the unknown. If teachers know whether students can accurately monitor their knowledge and thought processes and whether they can be taught memory monitoring of complex tasks, they can more ably facilitate students in the self-regulation of their own learning.

Learners can improve learning for the achievement of specific goals when they increase their awareness of their self-regulating capacity. By way of illustration, for the development of problem-solving skills across subject domains, Davidson *et al.* (1994) have identified four metacognitive processes that include:

- identifying and defining the problem;
- mentally representing the problem;
- planning how to proceed; and
- evaluating what you know about your performance.

Metacognitve theory focuses on those qualities of thinking that contribute to students' awareness and understanding of being self-regulatory and 'agents of their own thinking'. By developing curriculum, pedagogical and assessment practices that help students develop metacognitive processes, teachers can promote more profound learning opportunities and accomplishments for their students. It is through the processes of reflection and self-evaluation that are integral to developing a portfolio of work, that students' thinking about their own thinking can be enhanced. To illustrate, teachers can raise student awareness of metacognitve processes that are important in developing problem solving skills or they can discuss cognitive and motivational qualities of thinking. This information helps students become more conscious of these aspects in their own thinking when self-evaluating or reflecting on their own work. Such pedagogical practices can also foster student monitoring of their own learning and enhance student self-perception and motivation. Metacognition in this way can illuminate one's own thinking and develop independent learning. Teachers when they understand the way their students think and learn are more able to motivate, support and encourage their students' development in appropriate ways.

Paris and Winograd (1990: 28–9) identify four cognitive dimensions that influence students' orientations to learning. These are agency, instrumentality, control and purpose. The first dimension relates to how students perceive themselves as learners, say, for example, as competent or incompetent. These authors conclude that students' metacognitive beliefs must include the view that they are intentional, self-directed and self-critical learners. It is important that teachers foster this belief in students for their continuing success in learning. The second dimension concerns students' beliefs about the strategies they use and the achieved outcomes. To illustrate, students' views of the usefulness of certain strategies, such as summarising or note-taking, can impact on their achievements. The third dimension of control is associated with the students' understanding that they have the power to direct their own thinking. If this view is not developed then students will see themselves as ineffectual. The fourth dimension has to do with the students' beliefs about the purpose of their learning. Expectations should be positive and students need to value success. Paris and Winograd (1990) conclude that students' metacognitive beliefs about agency, instrumentality, control and purpose shape their orientations to learning. Some of the processes and principles that underpin the learning and pedagogy suited to the use of portfolios are intended to foster metacognitive awareness in these dimensions.

Reflective thinking and practice

Stenhouse (1975: 89) makes reference to Dewey's reflective theory of teaching: 'the active, careful and persistent examination of any belief, or purported form of knowledge, in the light of the grounds that support it and the further conclusions toward which it tends'. Such thinking is necessary in the development of a portfolio of work and requires a pedagogical approach not unlike that outlined by Stenhouse (1975). A process curriculum that develops this reflective capacity incorporates particular pedagogical principles. These principles have been expressed as pedagogical aims and are summarised below:

- to initiate and develop a process of question-posing (inquiry method);
- to teach research methodology where students look for information to answer questions that they have raised and use frameworks developed in the course to apply to new areas;
- to help students develop the ability to use a variety of first-hand sources as evidence from which to develop hypotheses and draw conclusions;
- to conduct discussions in which students learn to listen to others as well as express their own views;
- to legitimise the search, that is, give sanction and support to open-ended discussions where definitive answers to many questions are not found;
- to encourage students to reflect on their own experiences; and
- to create a new role for the teacher as a resource not an authority (Stenhouse, 1975: 92).

In the same light there are pedagogical implications for the development of reflexivity in the use of portfolios for assessment and learning purposes. Reflexivity or the capacity to review critically and reflectively one's own processes and practices of learning is fundamental to the portfolio process. Portfolios constitute reflections. The pedagogical approach that is needed requires teachers:

- to assist students in the inquiry of their own learning to identify their strengths and areas for improvement;
- to teach students about the importance of evidence and the quality of that evidence in relation to the particular purpose of the portfolio;
- to help students develop the ability to select evidence in relation to criteria and standards;
- to develop a constructive culture of critique;
- to provide opportunities for student constructions of learning to be validated;
- to encourage students to be reflective about their learning; and
- to facilitate learning and be a guide rather than a provider of information.

In a teacher-education context, Wolf (1991: 130) agrees with Shulman's observation, that portfolios 'retain almost uniquely the potential for documenting the unfolding of both teaching and learning over time and combining that documentation with opportunities for teachers to engage in the analysis of what they and their students have done'. The careful self-evaluation and monitoring of teaching and learning strategies by teachers provides quality information that can be used to examine growth and progress. Richert (1990: 524) in a study on the effect of particular aids to reflection in teacher education found that teachers felt the most significant reflection was that which occurred during the creation of their portfolios. It was when they were selecting materials for inclusion that they thought about what they did in their teaching and how well they did it, as well as what their materials were like, and how effective the materials were for their intended goals. Vavrus and Collins (1991: 24) also found that teachers engaging in the process of portfolio development appeared to become more reflective about their teaching practices 'particularly in terms of critiquing the effectiveness of instructional methods in addressing individual student's needs'. They found that when the contents of the portfolio were accompanied by reflective explanations, the complexity of teaching appeared to be captured. They also claimed that combinations of different types of documents such as examples of student work, video-tapes of teaching practice, lesson plans and teaching aids, helped to trace the development of teaching from planning through to practice and evaluation.

Lyons (1998b: 12) sees the portfolio in teacher education as a 'powerful reflective tool of professional and personal teacher growth and development'. She also sees the significance of the portfolio as a 'scaffolding for reflective teacher learning' (Lyons, 1998a: 5). She illustrates how the pre-service teacher 'finds in conversation an opportunity to look at and reflect on her experiences, to go beyond the entries of her portfolio, to see and make connections about her teaching, her students' learning, and the growth and development as a reflective practitioner' (Lyons, 1998c: 104).

In defining reflection Lyons refers to the work of Dewey (1933). He believed that reflective thinking involves: 'first, a state of doubt, hesitation, perplexity, mental difficulty, in which thinking originates and second, an act of searching, hunting, inquiring, to find material that will resolve the doubt, settle and dispose of the perplexity' (Lyons, 1998c: 106). Lyons suggests that reflective thinking for Dewey is 'deliberation'. Reference is also made to the work of Schön (1983, 1987, 1991) that highlighted that thought is embodied in action. 'Reflective practice comes into play in thinking in action, calling up all previous knowledge to address the particular situation of practice'. Lyons concludes that Schön's idea of knowledge-in-action, and Dewey's idea of 'deliberation', have become critical conceptual components for the knowledge of reflection.

Lyons makes reference to the work of Clarke (1995) which disputes the work of Schön and states that reflection occurs over time rather than in a single incident, and/or context. The focus of the reflection is the pre-service teachers' own constructions of meaning. In exploring the portfolio interview as a mode of fostering teacher reflection, Lyons supports Clarke's idea of reflection as thematic constructions of meaning, taking place over time and drawn from multiple experiences. Making connections between experiences, theory and practice, and constructing knowledge of teaching practice, constitutes reflection for Lyons.

Lyons concludes that reflective thinking is more like:

> a weaving, a threading together of experience, of making connections. This construction of meaning is in part directly in the service of making conscious

a teacher's knowledge of practice – a teaching philosophy, the sociopolitical or cultural contexts that influence the understanding of teaching or learning, and the understanding that the ethical may be a daily aspect of teaching. This takes place over time.

(1998c: 113)

Snyder *et al.* (1998) indicate that reflection is made possible in the portfolio process because there is a requirement to document thought and practice as they co-evolve. Students choose from a collection of work and reflect upon concrete evidence of their thinking and experiences at various points throughout their professional preparation year. This is how they can make their own growth visible to themselves. Snyder *et al.* (1998: 137) maintain that when students were allowed to fail they could articulate their growth: 'They built on their strengths and gained greater control over their own development, increased their motivation to keep failing (because anything worth doing, is worth doing wrong until you learn to do it right), and enhanced their potential for continual learning.'

Portfolios in teacher education: an exemplar

Research findings (Shulman, 1998; Lyons, 1998a) suggest that when students create their portfolios they develop important skills such as critique, reflection and self-evaluation for development and improvement of learning. When students put the portfolio of work together they select relevant evidence that addresses specific knowledge, skills and understandings of the learning domain. They need to understand and be able to develop criteria to determine the quality of the evidence they select. Different data can be collected for thorough documentation of attitudes (changes in beliefs and values relative to the subject), behaviours, achievement, improvements, thinking, reflection and self-evaluation. In this process they are encouraged to produce their best work and value progress. This process of portfolio development helps to validate students' constructed meanings. The context of teacher education will be used here as an exemplar of the wider value of the portfolio.

The portfolio has the potential to provide a structure and processes for documenting, reflecting and making public learning and teaching practices. Learning and teaching are complex activities. The use of a portfolio to capture and illustrate development, particularly in teacher education, has gained momentum, especially in the United States of America. The inclusion of process artefacts in the portfolio and their use in the development of reflective practice is a significant gain in the teacher-education context.

Teaching has been described as a complex, multifaceted activity that requires a variety of complex, multifaceted assessments (King, 1991). The use of portfolios for assessment can more accurately portray the complexity, depth and scope of teaching and learning. This is one of numerous reasons why portfolios are advocated in the context of teacher education.

Wolf *et al.* (1995) summarise the varying teaching contexts where teaching portfolios have been implemented. These include teacher-education programmes with pre-service teachers, induction programmes for beginning teachers, with practising teachers in subject-matter projects, in school district pay-for-performance plans, with teacher re-licensure at the state level, in national efforts to certify accomplished practitioners and with university faculties in higher education. As Wolf *et al.* (1995: 30) conclude, while the contexts vary the purpose of the portfolio remains the same; that is 'to improve teacher effectiveness'.

The method of assessment used in teacher education should clearly be chosen to promote the intended outcomes. For pre-service teachers it also needs to support the acquisition of professional attitudes and to develop strategies of reflective thinking and critical self-evaluation. The intended learning outcomes in teacher education include:

- development of reflective thinking;
- increased awareness of learning and teaching styles;
- development of one's own values and philosophy of education;
- expanded knowledge;
- increased professionalism;
- awareness of high standards and professional standards;
- self-evaluation for improvement purposes;
- promotion of student learning;
- provision of stimulating and challenging learning environments; and
- use of authentic learning and assessment.

Such a broad range of learning outcomes requires assessment that will provide ample opportunity for the development, practice and evaluation of these skills, understandings and attitudes. The portfolio provides a structure for documenting and reflecting on teaching and learning practice. The processes and procedures for the development of a portfolio enable the pre-service teacher to demonstrate achievements and competencies. For instance, the pre-service teacher collects evidence from a range of tasks and information about teaching over time in different settings. A richer portrayal of teaching practice is possible. The collection of evidence in the portfolio, together with reflective statements, can provide meaningful insights into teaching, and a more representative sample of performance, than a one-off observation.

Research (Vavrus and Collins, 1991) on the use of portfolios for assessment purposes in teacher education has found that the experience of developing a portfolio requires processes that facilitate the development of the following skills and understandings:

- higher-order skills (problem-solving, analysis, synthesis, evaluation, creativity);
- self-assessment and critique of own work, teaching, and learning experiences;
- understanding of own learning processes;
- self-regulation and self-direction in own learning;
- reflectivity through examination of own beliefs and concepts;
- enhanced professional identity and skills;

- growth and commitment to that growth;
- personal control through taking responsibility and ownership of own work;
- understanding and use of own strengths and successes (important for adult learners); and
- appropriate professional behaviour through continuous learning and role-modelling.

The portfolio approach to assessment impacts on curriculum and pedagogy so that the assessment interactions between lecturers and pre-service teachers are promoted around the collection of work. Wolf et al. (1995: 31) indicate that teaching portfolios might engender individual reflection and improve practice, however, 'their value in promoting teaching effectiveness are more likely to dramatically increase when they serve as the focal point for conversations with colleagues about teaching'. Wolf et al. (1995: 31) refer to the work of Shulman, who has indicated that to achieve the full value of the teaching portfolio it must become 'a departure point *for substantive conversations* about the quality of a teacher's work'. Portfolio use for assessment in teacher education supports the current emphasis on meaning in learning and the need for the learner to adopt an active role in the learning process

While the focus at the end of this chapter has been on portfolio use in teacher education, portfolios are also used in other contexts for learning and assessment purposes. As stressed in the previous chapter there are many portfolios used for a range of purposes in the contexts of primary, secondary, further and higher education.

The type of portfolio is dependent on the particular purpose and audience for which it will be used. What is common to all types of portfolios are the processes which include critical self-evaluation, substantive dialogue, interview or learning conversation during the compilation of the portfolio and/or the presentation of the evidence, reflection about one's own practice and/or learning throughout portfolio development. These learning and associated pedagogical processes can help to facilitate metacognitive development.

Summary

- The development of a portfolio of work involves key learning processes such as self-evaluation, substantive conversation, reflective thinking and practice.
- These learning processes and associated pedagogic practices, when used to develop a portfolio of work, foster metacognitive development which promotes knowing how, when, where and why one learns.
- In teacher education portfolios are used increasingly because they provide a structure and processes for documenting, reflecting and making public learning and teaching practices.

3 Key concepts in portfolio assessment

The development of a portfolio of work involves personal engagement with important learning processes and an opportunity for the learner to achieve a 'personally unique accomplishment'. For as stated by Stake:

> Knowing the rank order of students as to proficiency is not at all the same as knowing what students know . . . Education is not so much as achieving of some fixed standard. In a true sense, it requires unique and personal definition for each learner . . . Education is a personal process and a personally unique accomplishment.
>
> (Stake quoted in Mabry, 1999: 26)

The evidence in the portfolio can reflect a diverse collection of measures (or ways to assess student progress) and process artefacts that capture a unique picture of how much and how well an individual has learned. The kinds of evidence can include performance assessments, open-ended items, projects, assignments, essays, tests, records, profiles, self-evaluations, reflective statements, video- or audio-tapes. As discussed in chapter 1, a portfolio of work can be used to monitor progress or as a summative assessment tool. The collection of evidence provides insights into what knowledge and skills are required for the individual to move forward and can also indicate what has been achieved. The range of purposes for portfolio use together with the possibility of submitting such a variety of assessment data to reflect learning have important professional development implications for teachers and assessors. Knowledge of assessment, understanding of the relationship of assessment and curriculum and recognition of the importance of assessment for learning are essential if portfolios are to be used for assessment and learning profitably. Assessing a portfolio of work is a more complex process than simply ascribing a grade. When judging the contents of a portfolio a confidence with certain assessment concepts becomes fundamental. For reporting purposes much more than a grade, percentile or rank is required. The aim of this chapter is to discuss the key assessment concepts that need to be understood at various phases of portfolio design and development.

At the outset it must be understood that a particular portfolio assessment procedure will not be valid in every situation. Portfolios used for ongoing formative purposes focus on the improvement of learning. Those used for summative assessments for accountability purposes are guided by externally prescribed requirements for the measurement of how well students and schools or institutions have achieved agreed standards and to provide information for certification and selection. Each type of portfolio requires an assessment procedure that fits its particular purpose. These assessment procedures allow the student to demonstrate what he or she knows and can do and are reliant on qualitative judgements of performance. For assessors to be proficient and confident in making such judgements much support in terms of assessor professional development and guidance are required.

Assessors require an understanding of essential assessment concepts to ensure that the procedures and processes adopted are aligned with the intended purpose of the portfolio. This chapter describes key assessment concepts related to using portfolios for learning and assessment. These concepts are presented according to developmental phases and uses of portfolios.

- phase one: conceptualisation of portfolios to support the learning and teaching processes;
- phase two: construction and development of portfolios to support teaching and learning processes; and
- phase three: grading of portfolios for summative purposes (see Figure 3.1).

Concepts such as developmental assessment (that incorporates progress maps and developmental continua) and criterion referencing are important to consider at the outset of the portfolio design and these are discussed first. During the development phase of a portfolio of work assessment concepts such as formative

Figure 3.1 Developmental framework of key assessment concepts for portfolios

Phase one: Conceptualisation of the portfolio
- Developmental assessment
- Developmental continua
- Progress maps
- Criterion referencing

        Phase two: Development of the portfolio
        - Formative assessment
        - Feedback
        - Performance assessment
        - Validity

                Phase three: Grading of the portfolio
                - Reliability
                - Standards
                - Summative assessment
                - Holistic assessment

assessment, feedback, performance assessment and validity (content, construct and consequential aspects) are important for the teacher or assessor. When a portfolio is submitted for final assessment and grading purposes reliability, standards and summative assessment are particularly relevant. The processes involved in assessing the portfolio holistically, for summative assessment purposes, are dealt with at the conclusion of this chapter. These processes are unique to the procedure of assessing multiple entries such as those included in a portfolio of work and differ from evaluating a single test, assignment or text.

The assessment concepts identified in this chapter illustrate changing emphases and parallel the characteristics of the 'modernisation of curriculum and assessment' (Torrance, 1997). This shift in assessment corresponds to changes in theories of learning, curriculum and pedagogy. Figure 3.2 shows how Torrance views these changes.

Assessment

Assessment as used in this book is considered as an integral aspect of the teaching and learning cycle and can include a range of methods for monitoring and evaluating student performance and attainment. These methods range from formal testing and examinations, performance assessments including practical and oral presentations, teacher- or classroom-based assessment and portfolios. The assessment data in a portfolio can include formal written tests or examinations, practical and oral assessments, evaluation of classroom activities, marking of performances, profiles, target-setting and self-assessments. Assessment as it applies to the portfolio is best understood as an interpretive process (Griffin, 1998b: 5). This interpretation of students' learning is based on 'evidence from what students write, do, say, create or make'. Griffin refers to these as categories of evidence used for the assessment of learning. The inferences drawn from these observable data lead to decisions about progress and development and are used to support and predict future learning. The nature of the evidence is crucial, for the better the evidence on which such

Figure 3.2 Changing emphases in assessment

Shift from	Towards
Assessing knowledge	Assessing skills and understandings
Assessing products	Assessing processes
External end of course assessment	Internal during course assessment
Written assessments only	Use of a variety of methods and evidence
Norm-referencing	Criterion referencing
Pass/fail summative assessment	Formative identification of strengths and weaknesses and recording of positive achievement

Source: Torrance (1997).

judgements are based the more likely the teacher or assessor will make accurate or valid inferences of a student's achievement.

In addition assessment can be defined as:

> A general term embracing all methods customarily used to appraise performance of an individual pupil or group. It may refer to a broad appraisal including many sources of evidence and many aspects of a pupil's knowledge, understanding, skills and attitudes; or to a particular occasion or instrument. An assessment instrument may be any method or procedure, formal or informal, for producing information about pupils: for example, a written test paper, an interview schedule, a measurement task using equipment, a class quiz.
>
> (Black, 1998: 5)

The portfolio is a more 'expansionist' form of assessment as it allows multiple sources of evidence and a range of assessment measures to be incorporated into the portfolio collection.

Gipps (1997: 13) has indicated that good assessment practice should:

- support learning and reflection, including formative assessment;
- be open and connected to clear criteria rather than be linked to comparative performance of others; and
- include a range of assessment strategies so that all learners have a chance to perform well.

Assessment tasks need to involve a variety of contexts, range of modes within the assessment, range of response formats and styles to achieve the latter goal as outlined by Gipps. There is also a need to expand the range of indicators used to provide an opportunity for those who might be disadvantaged by one form of assessment to offer alternative evidence of their expertise. Portfolios offer students the opportunity to benefit from assessment practices that meet Gipps's requirements.

More recently the Assessment Reform Group (1999) in England has identified the following characteristics of assessment for learning:

- views assessment as an essential part of teaching and learning;
- involves sharing learning goals with pupils;
- aims to help pupils know the standards aimed for;
- involves pupils in self assessment;
- provides feedback that helps take learning forward;
- is underpinned by confidence that every pupil can improve;
- involves teachers and pupils in reviewing assessment data.

Assessment for learning as characterised here underpins the approach to portfolio use as suggested in this book. The processes integral to the development of the portfolio reflect these characteristics. The implication is that there are key assessment concepts that need to be understood if teachers are to feel confident in the use of portfolios for assessment and learning.

Competence

Assessment and teaching are integrated in the process of portfolio development. The work contained in the portfolio can reflect evidence of change and provides the teacher with information for assessment and for feedback that takes learning forward. It is possible for learning to be improved through teacher guidance and self-instruction. Glaser (1990: 476) makes reference to the work of Hatch and Gardner who suggest that students' portfolios can be assessed in terms of different dimensions such as: 'conceptualisation, presentation, competence, individuality and co-operation'.

Glaser outlines characteristics that differentiate the performance of experts from novices. He suggests that 'as proficiency develops, knowledge becomes increasingly integrated, new forms of cognitive skill emerge, access to knowledge is swift, and the efficiency of the performance is heightened' (1990: 477). Such changes are used to define criteria for assessment of competence. Glaser describes how demonstration of increased competence in a domain will reflect a knowledge base that is increasingly 'coherent, principled, useful and goal-oriented'. If a portfolio of work is constructed and assessed using a developmental approach it is possible to capture such evidence that reflects growth in competence.

Glaser (1990: 477) outlines each of these criteria. As individuals attain competence, elements of knowledge are interconnected and there is growth in 'structuredness of the information, coherence, and accessibility to interrelated knowledge'. Proficient individuals access coherent 'chunks' when they perform a task. In contrast, a novice is likely to demonstrate superficial understanding because information is less integrated. The second criterion to be used to assess competence is described by Glaser (1990: 477) as 'principled problem solving' or the way a problem is interpreted to enable the completion of the task. Proficient individuals are able to identify underlying principles and patterns while a novice is only able to deal with the surface features of a problem.

'Usable knowledge' or 'the progression from declarative to procedural and goal-oriented information' is the third criterion for assessment of competence, as defined by Glaser. He describes how knowledge is acquired by accumulating facts 'in declarative or propositional form, to their compilation in condition-action form'. He explains how novices might know a principle or a rule but are unable to use the knowledge effectively while proficient individuals access their knowledge and know the conditions of applicability. Glaser concludes that experts and novices may be equally competent at recalling specific items of information, but the more experienced relate these items to 'the goals of problem solution and conditions for action'.

Self-regulatory skills (Glaser, 1990) involve the ability to:

- monitor performance;

- check the appropriateness of strategies;
- judge the difficulty of a task;
- apportion time;
- ask questions about the task;
- assess the relevance of knowledge; and
- predict the outcomes of performance.

The acquisition of these skills helps to enhance knowledge.

When assessment is integrated with teaching and learning there is more opportunity for the individual to receive guidance and support in developing competence. Glaser argues that assessment should focus on competence essential to future learning rather than only indicate current or past achievement. He concludes that mastery of skills and knowledge of a domain should be viewed as 'enabling competencies for the future'. This attitude of enablement is helpful in motivating us to assess knowledge in terms of its constructive use for further action. When considering the assessment of the portfolio this principle is fundamental and relates to developmental assessment.

Developmental assessment

In conceptualising the portfolio to support learning and teaching processes developmental assessment (with the use of developmental continua and progress maps) becomes fundamental. This is because the portfolio documents achievements over an extended period of time and learning is demonstrated from an accumulated collection of work. Assessment needs to be designed developmentally and integrated with the curriculum. Criterion referencing is also an important assessment concept at this phase of design.

Masters (1997: 1) defines developmental assessment as 'the process of monitoring students' progress through an area of learning so that decisions can be made about the best ways to facilitate further learning'. The purpose of developmental assessment is to judge a student's attainment on a progress map, developmental continuum or set of descriptors of progress, to identify the learning experiences appropriate to the identified stage in the student's learning and to monitor the student's learning over time. A progress map is a description of skills, understandings and knowledge outlined in a developmental sequence. The essential distinguishing feature of developmental assessment is the monitoring of progress against described continua (Masters, 1997). Developmental continua are best exemplified in the 'First Steps' and 'Stepping Out' literacy frameworks that link assessment with teaching and learning. These frameworks were researched and developed by the Education Department of Western Australia. The 'First Steps' programme covers the four areas of oral language, reading, writing and spelling. For each of these areas a developmental continuum has been prepared to identify the phases in a child's development from pre-literacy to independence. For purposes of illustration only, a summary of the 'Spelling Developmental Continuum' will be given in Figure 3.3.

Figure 3.3 A summary of the 'First Steps Developmental Continuum for Spelling'

Developmental continuum – a summary
Spelling
Phase one: Preliminary spelling
Phase two: Semi-phonetic spelling
Phase three: Phonetic spelling
Phase four: Transitional spelling
Phase five: Independent spelling
Note: These phases are not to be equated with school grade/year levels.

Source: Education Department of Western Australia (1996).

What is important to understand is that the 'First Steps' materials were developed 'to give teachers an explicit way of mapping children's progress through observation' (Education Department of Western Australia, 1996: 2). Another aim of providing teachers with developmental continua is to validate what teachers know about children and to present them 'with a way of looking at what children can actually do and how they can do it, in order to inform planning for further development' (ibid.). The continua are derived from research into the development of literacy in English speaking children. Key indicators have been identified and presented in phases to allow teachers to map overall progress and also to demonstrate that children's language does not develop in a linear sequence. Individual children can demonstrate a range of indicators from any of the phases at any one time. The rationale for the identification of the 'key' indicators is to place children within a specific phase so that links can be made to appropriate learning experiences. A 'unique and personal definition' for each child is possible by including developmental records in a child's portfolio. For as suggested to teachers in the 'First Steps Spelling Developmental Continuum':

> Developmental records show that children seldom progress in a neat and well-sequenced manner; instead they may remain in one phase for some length of time and move rapidly through other phases. Each child is a unique individual . . . so that no two developmental pathways are the same.
>
> (Ibid.)

To demonstrate more specifically the nature of developmental continuum the key indicators for only phases one and two are presented in Figure 3.4 with *some* detail of other descriptors of behaviour for each of these phases. Teachers are reminded in the guidelines that:

> *The indicators are not designed to provide evaluative criteria through which every child is expected to progress in sequential order.*
>
> (Ibid.)

Figure 3.4 'First Steps Spelling Developmental Continuum' showing key indicators for phases one and two *only* and *some* additional indicators

Indicators for spelling developmental continuum Teachers can identify a child's phase of development by observing that the child is exhibiting all the key indicators of a phase. It should be noted however, that most children will also display indicators from other phases.	Student's name _____ I.D. _____ School _____
Phase one: Preliminary spelling In this phase children become aware that print carries a message. They experiment with writing-like symbols as they try to represent written language. Their writing is not readable by others as understandings of sound–symbol relationships have yet to develop.	**Phase two: Semi-phonetic spelling** In this phase children show developing understanding of sound–symbol relationships. Their spelling attempts show some evidence of sound–symbol correspondence. They may represent a whole word with one, two or three letters.
Key indicators ♦ is aware that print carries a message	**Key indicators** ♦ uses left to right and top to bottom orientation of print
♦ uses writing like symbols to represent written language	• relies on the sounds which are most obvious to him or her. This may be the initial sound, initial and final sounds, or initial, medial and final sounds, e.g. D (down), DN (down), DON (down), KT (kitten), WT (went), BAB (baby), LRFT (elephant)
♦ uses known letters or approximations of letters to represent written language	♦ represents a whole word with one, two or three letters. Uses mainly consonants, e.g. KGR (kangaroo), BT (bit)
♦ assigns a message to own symbols	• uses an initial letter to represent most words in a sentence, e.g. s o i s g to c a s (Someone is going to climb a slide)
• knows that writing and drawing are different	• uses letter names to represent sounds, syllables or words, e.g. AT (eighty)
• knows that a word can be written down	• uses a combination of consonants with a vowel related to a letter name, e.g. GAM (game), MI (my)
• draws symbols that resemble letters using straight, curved and intersecting lines	• writes one or two letters for sounds, then adds random letters to complete the word, e.g. greim (grass), rdms (radio)

Source: Education Department of Western Australia (1996).

This developmental view of teaching and learning considers the contexts in which development takes place and acknowledges that children's achievements form a pattern of development that contains a wide range of individual difference.

The construction of a progress map or a learning continuum is a preliminary step in implementing developmental assessment (Masters, 1997). Teachers, through their experience of teaching, understand how the development of learning in a particular area usually occurs. These indicators of attainment are outlined and then tested. The framework developed helps teachers think about and monitor student progress in the particular area of learning.

Evidence, including observations, can be collected in a portfolio that is designed for developmental purposes. Teachers make systematic recordings of observations and judgements during their classroom teaching. They develop particular strategies for recording achievement, for observations of student classroom behaviour and assigned classroom work. This evidence is then used to identify, according to best fit, the level of the student's attainment on the progress map. Comments on ways to improve are recorded directly on to work as feedback to students and can be included in the portfolio.

In Western Australia the implementation of an outcomes-based curriculum for compulsory years of schooling (K-10) (aged five to fifteen) has required the development of standards of student performance in each learning area. The eight areas are: the arts, English, health and physical education, languages other than English, mathematics, science, society and environment and technology and enterprise. Eight levels are identified and represent the typical milestones of student achievement. They are not related to age or year of schooling but are representative of the compulsory years of schooling. For each learning area, key dimensions are identified and illustrative descriptions of ways students might demonstrate performance in relation to particular curriculum outcome statements are presented. These descriptions are not prescriptive or exhaustive.

To illustrate the developmental nature of the outcomes and standards framework developed by the Education Department of Western Australia, the learning area of Society and Environment will be used. For this learning area the student outcome statements describe increasing levels of sophistication that students typically demonstrate as they actively explore and make sense of their society and environment. These outcome statements are organised into six strands:

- investigation, communication and participation;
- place and space;
- resources;
- culture;
- time, continuity and change;
- natural and social systems (Education Department of Western Australia, 1997b: 70).

For the 'Society and Environment Student Outcome Statement for the Investigation, Communication and Participation' strand, the 'Foundation Outcome

Statements' (FOS) and the eight levels will be illustrated for one of the sub-strands, 'Planning Investigations' (see Figure 3.5).

Teachers are provided with suggested types of evidence that can inform decisions related to the assessment of students' performance. They are also provided with an illustration of how to record achievement. Such recorded evidence can be used to assess the student's development on a progress map. The validity of the assessment is dependent on the relevance of the recorded evidence. The recorded evidence or observations need to represent the range of outcomes indicated on the progress map for that learning area and need to reflect adequately the student's abilities. The evidence needs to be comprised of 'fair' indicators of achievement without student characteristics, such as gender or cultural background, impacting on attainment.

Figure 3.5 'Society and Environment' levels and foundation outcome statements for the sub-strand of 'Planning Investigations' of the 'Investigation, Communication and Participation' strand.

Strand: Investigation, Communication and Participation		
Sub-strand: Planning Investigations Students critically review and reflect on their understandings, formulate questions as a focus for investigation, predict possible answers or formulate hypotheses and design suitable methods for organising and gathering information.		
The student:		
FOS	ICP F.1	Displays interest in people and places.
Level 1	ICP 1.1	Contributes relevant ideas and suggestions from their direct experience or from a stimulus provided.
Level 2	ICP 2.1	Identifies, given a focus question, some of the factors to be considered in a familiar social/environmental context.
Level 3	ICP 3.1	Plans an investigation for a topic, by identifying possible sources of information and making simple predictions based on personal experiences.
Level 4	ICP 4.1	Identifies the types of observations, data and sources appropriate to a topic and decides how they will be used to gain information.
Level 5	ICP 5.1	Analyses a social/environmental issue, formulates questions and plans ways of investigating them.
Level 6	ICP 6.1	Analyses a problem, formulates their own hypothesis, uses social and environmental conceptual understandings to identify the main aspects to be considered and makes predictions.
Level 7	ICP 7.1	Independently devises one or more research tasks or hypotheses to guide the investigation of an issue or event.
Level 8	ICP 8.1	Presents a research proposal and designs a research plan using the methodologies of social and environmental inquiry.

Source: Education Department of Western Australia (1997b: 72).

The reliability of the assessment depends on the amount of evidence that is used to estimate the level of achievement. When the student's attainment is located on a progress map, procedures are required that consider the specifics of the tasks that the individual student attempts and the contexts in which these tasks are performed.

For reporting purposes the progress map describes the skills, knowledge and understandings typically demonstrated by students. The location of the particular student's attainment is indicated on the developmental continuum. These descriptions are used for teacher–student or teacher–parent discussions of progress. It is at this stage that the kinds of learning activities that are likely to be most useful to improve a student's learning are identified.

The information given to teachers to help them assess their students' performance is in the form of illustrative descriptions of ways students might demonstrate performance. These are called pointers and are neither prescriptive nor exhaustive. The teacher will assess the student's learning by looking for best fit. To show the detail provided an example will be given in Figure 3.6 from the 'Investigation, Communication and Participation' strand for the learning area of 'Society and Environment' for levels 1 and 2 *only*.

Developmental assessment underpins the curriculum design as illustrated here for the 'First Steps' literacy programme and the Education Department of Western Australia's Student Outcome Statements. The use of developmental continua and progress maps help the teacher plan for further development. Evidence collected in a portfolio of work will include examples of work that illustrates the particular phase or level of development of the individual according to best fit. In summing up this section on developmental assessment the principles that Masters (1997) has described to define this type of assessment will be given:

- use of a progress map or developmental continuum;
- individuals' levels of attainment are estimated and located on this map;
- a wide range of evidence is used to assess students' achievements;
- interpretations of levels of achievement are described in terms of knowledge, skills and understandings typical of students at each level;
- achievements are displayed graphically indicating a student's estimated location on the map; and
- numbers are only used to mark students' estimated levels of achievement.

To incorporate these principles into assessment practice teachers need a substantial level of support in the form of exemplars, training and resources to accompany the use of the developmental continuum or progress maps. This level of support is provided in the 'First Steps' and 'Stepping Out' literacy programmes and helps to develop consistency and standardisation in practice.

Developmental assessment is reliant on formative assessment and feedback that is given during teacher–student conversations or conferences about work in the portfolio. This work is used to assess a student's performance according to the progress map or developmental continuum. The use of formative assessment helps

Figure 3.6 Level 1 and 2 illustrative descriptions of ways students might demonstrate performance for the sub-strand of 'Planning Investigations' of the 'Investigation, Communication and Participation' strand for the learning area of 'Society and Environment'

Strand: Investigation, Communication and Participation	
Sub-strand: Planning Investigations	
Level 1	**Level 2**
ICP 1.1 Contributes relevant ideas and suggestions from their direct experience or from a stimulus provided	**ICP 2.1** Given a focus question, identify some of the factors to be considered in a familiar social/environmental context.
This will be evident when students, for example: • talk about a topic using information from their own experience or a stimulus such as picture, film or story • formulate simple literal questions to gather specific information to seek clarification	*This will be evident when students, for example:* • participate in a group brainstorm to identify the key concepts and the associated language for a topic • describe what is going to be investigated and how they will collect information • design both literal and inferential questions to seek literal and factual information to clarify the needs for a given topic • design questions to ask groups or individuals on a given topic • with teacher assistance cooperate with people they are comfortable with to use techniques for encouraging creative ideas (e.g. De Bono's Possible, Potential, Perhaps strategy, brainstorming) • negotiate group rules and follow them (e.g. use strategies to ensure everyone's views are heard)

Source: Education Department of Western Australia (1997b: 74–5).

to identify the student's achievement and to plan future learning. For Harlen and James (1997) formative assessment is being aware of a student's existing ideas and skills, analysing his or her development and indicating the next steps forward. They have indicated that although descriptions of attainment in the National Curriculum in England and Wales provided criteria for teachers to assess pupils' achievements, by deciding the level reached, the genuinely formative use of assessment was neglected. When portfolios are designed for developmental purposes it is fundamental that the teacher not only indicates the level attained but provides the student with feedback that will help him or her understand how to improve and what to do to take the learning forward.

It is useful at this stage to remind the reader of the distinction between criteria and standards. Criteria are the dimensions or characteristics upon which the judgement of the student performance is made; the standards are the levels of quality applying along a developmental scale. Criterion referencing and the use of criteria in relation to portfolios will now be considered more specifically because of the important implications for the conceptualisation phase of the portfolio.

Criterion referencing

In differentiating between criterion- and norm-referenced measures in the 1960s Glaser (1963: 519) indicated that the former are dependent upon 'an absolute standard of quality' while norm-referenced measures 'depend upon a relative standard'. The underlying concept of achievement measurement was described as 'a continuum of knowledge acquisition ranging from no proficiency at all to perfect performance'. An assessor could indicate a level at a point on this continuum from an assessment of the evidence. Criterion-referenced measures of achievement are used to assess the degree to which the student's achievement resembles desired performance at any specified level. Glaser (1963: 520) concluded that measures which assess student achievement in terms of criterion standard provide information about 'the degree of competence attained by a particular student, which is independent of reference to the performance of others'. Griffin (1998a: 7) suggests that during the 1970s: 'the mastery/non mastery interpretation reduced assessment to a level of trivia and checklists of unrelated and non-coherent sets of skills'. In the 1980s Griffin explains that Glaser expanded his original description of criterion referencing by conceiving assessment of tasks as ordered coherent sets that could be referenced to stages on a continuum of increasing competence, which facilitated an overall interpretation of attainment.

This principle underpins the developmental nature of portfolio assessment systems. A continuum of increasing competence is used to assess a student's development. The assessment is dependent on the tasks performed and the manner in which the tasks are undertaken. The performance and the task are interpreted by their relative positions on a continuum. Figure 3.7 illustrates this type of continuum of the use of text forms from the 'Stepping Out' literacy programme of the Education Department of Western Australia. Key indicators identify relevant behaviours for six levels. Teachers use these to determine the student's position on the continuum according to best fit as apparent from the quality of recorded evidence in the portfolio.

Criteria

The use of explicit criteria provides a schema for assessing performance and helps to establish teaching goals and curriculum expectations. To develop assessment criteria requires an understanding of what constitutes quality in performance and

Figure 3.7 Extract from the 'Stepping Out' literacy programme of the Education
Department of Western Australia

Continuum of the use of text forms	
Level	Key indicators
1	Writing and speaking shows little or no organising framework.
2	Uses some organising framework in a limited range of forms such as personal recounts, simple procedures, simple reports and brief imaginary stories.
3	Composes simply a limited number of text forms to suit different purposes and audiences. Uses appropriate structures when composing in a limited range of forms which includes narratives, recounts, procedures and reports. Includes for example: • aspects of setting and an extended plot in a narrative; • most significant facts when reporting on familiar topics; • includes most steps when explaining a simple procedure; • important events are elaborated in a personal recount.
4	Develops ideas in a range of forms to suit different purposes and audiences. Uses and sustains the appropriate structures in a range of forms which include simple explanations and expositions. Includes for example: • all the aspects when explaining a procedure; • brief arguments to support an opinion in an exposition; • a complication (conflict) which is resolved in a narrative.
5	When writing or speaking about accessible topics, meets all the organisational requirements of a wide range of text forms. Includes for example: • expositions that contain a thesis, well-developed arguments and a restatement of the thesis; • narratives that include effective characterisation, and elaborated plots; • sequenced and clearly elaborated steps in a procedure.
6	When writing about complex topics, uses all the organisational requirements of a wide range of text forms to develop, support and control ideas for a variety of purposes and audiences. Includes for example: • well developed and supported arguments for a general audience in an extended exposition; • arguments for and against which are clearly presented, developed and supported in an explanation; • sustained descriptions of the steps in a complex process in an explanation.

Source: Education Department of Western Australia (1997c).

implies expertise in the particular content area. The processes of portfolio development require students to self-evaluate and to select evidence for inclusion in the
portfolio dependent on its purpose. This is a fundamental reason for sharing with
the student the concept and the various types of criteria. A shared understanding
of the criteria and the standards can be gained when the teacher engages the
student in substantive dialogue about the work selected for the portfolio and
the self-evaluations of that work.

The mechanistic use of criteria is not being advocated. Rather, what is being
suggested is that students first, together with their teachers or peers, need to
understand the concept of criteria: that is, the characteristics or dimensions on
which the quality of performance is judged. Secondly they need to understand
what these dimensions or characteristics are. This understanding occurs from
interactive dialogue with peers and teacher feedback that takes learning forward.
Finally students need to understand the standards or the levels of excellence
expressed in terms of differentiation of quality. This understanding is gained from
feedback about their own work in relation to the standards. It is in this context that
students also need to understand the various types of criteria, and the importance
of emergent criteria, so that the unintended consequences of the use of explicit
criteria can be avoided.

Mabry (1999) warns that the rigid use of explicit criteria for assessment of a
portfolio of work can be detrimental. This is because flexibility, on the part of the
assessor, such as considering the unique or particular qualities of a student's work
may not occur. She states: 'when the student's work must be judged according to
the criteria and not on its own merits, when the criteria are not well related to what
the student has done, the student is likely to be undercredited for his or her
accomplishment' (ibid.: 58).

The use of explicit criteria can also lead to what Mabry expresses as: 'teaching
to the rubric . . . a dismaying variation on the theme of teaching to the test' (ibid.).
When teachers discuss the criteria for assessment and make them explicit
for their students the implication for students is that their performance should
conform to these. What can result from this process is the unintended consequence
of the standardisation of students' performances. The stifling of creativity and of
the uniqueness of personal learning accomplishment is a serious deleterious
consequence that is unhelpful.

Mabry (1999: 59) has identified three types of criteria according to when and
who develops them and describes the advantages and disadvantages of each type.
Preordinate criteria are determined at the outset before learning takes place and
prior to the assessment of that learning. A disadvantage of preordinate criteria is
that they can focus assessment so that unique or creative qualities of the student's
work can be overlooked. Mabry (1999: 60) argues that students who meet the
criteria superficially could 'get higher scores than [those] who do better substantive
work but in a way the criteria failed to anticipate'.

Emergent criteria are determined during learning or assessment in response to a
quality that is valued and becomes evident from direct experience or during the
performance. Emergent criteria provide the opportunity for teachers to respond to

changes in the lessons and actual learning. They can arise during actual student performance and can be stated during the lesson or during assessment when unanticipated qualities of student work are exhibited and worthy of recognition. Here Mabry (1999: 60) argues that 'assessment is related to the curriculum as experienced rather than the curriculum as planned'.

Negotiated criteria are determined by students and teachers (or assessors) and provide the opportunity for students to think about what is important or of value about their own work. These criteria allow students the opportunity to articulate what they believe to be important. This experience helps them develop personal standards of quality and promotes responsibility for their own learning. Mabry (1999: 61) makes the important point: 'for criteria to be truly negotiated, assessors must be willing to share authority with students . . . assessors must really listen and work to incorporate students' ideas into the assessment'.

Not everything in the portfolio will be assessed using the same level of criteria. To illustrate, consider the personal studies folio of work for candidates studying Higher Grade English in Scotland, described in chapter 1. This folio of work consists of two pieces of coursework in reading and writing undertaken during the year of presentation. These pieces consist of a review of personal reading and either a piece of imaginative or discursive writing. The criteria for the review of personal reading include:

- personal stance;
- line of thought;
- knowledge of text;
- textual analysis (style/structure);
- linguistic/literary/mass media awareness, where appropriate (Scottish Examination Board, 1991: 5).

For the assessment of the creative writing included in the folio the following axiological criteria are used:

- theme/content;
- structure/form;
- stance/tone/mood;
- expression/style (Scottish Examination Board, 1992: 6).

It is this level of criteria that allows for the emergence of criteria that capture originality and creativity in the performance or demonstration of learning. As apparent from this example, it is possible for different entries of the portfolio to be assessed using different levels and types of criteria. What is also apparent is that the different contexts need to be considered in the assessment of student performance and attainment.

In Scotland there is substantial support provided for the student and the teacher in the form of exemplars and guidance to assist in the development and assessment of work.

Formative assessment

Torrance and Pryor (1998) indicate that in general formative assessment takes place during a course and is intended to improve student learning. This complex process can be teacher-centred where teachers take on the role of providing students with feedback that indicates the extent to which specific aspects of learning have been attained with the aim of helping students to improve on their subsequent performances. The other view is one that sees students assuming an active role by reflecting on what has been accomplished and how this has been achieved.

This difference in emphasis of student and teacher roles in the process of formative assessment is particularly important. In the processes outlined for the development of a portfolio, student understanding of and reflection on the process is valued. Torrance and Pryor (1998: 10) also support this position and define formative assessment as: 'a construct, a name that is given to what should more accurately be characterized as a social interaction between teacher and pupil which is intended to have a positive impact on pupil learning, but may not'. This definition aligns with Vygotsky's theory that cognition is socially situated and develops in a dynamic and interactive way.

As indicated in chapter 2 the learner has a central role in the portfolio process. This is also true for the learner's role in formative assessment. In order for assessment to function formatively, results have to be used to adjust teaching and learning – that is, feedback that students receive on their achievements, strengths or areas for improvement from their teachers or peers must have a transformative function. This form of assessment takes place during the process of developing work for inclusion in the portfolio, not when the work for the portfolio is completed. Formative assessment is developmental and aims to identify areas for remediation so that subsequent instruction, study and progress can take place. Sadler (1989) in explaining the learner's role in formative assessment indicates that teachers need to discuss the required standards and indicate strategies for improvement so students can be self-monitoring.

The implication is that it is just as important for the student to monitor his or her own process of learning as it is for the teacher. As has been argued a portfolio approach can assist in this learning process. It involves formative assessment that supports learning, and involves teacher–student interaction as part of the assessment process itself. This conception of formative assessment links to a view of learning that sees student development as multidimensional not sequential and based on stimulus–response theories (Sadler, 1989).

Formative assessment has an important role in relation to learning with understanding or deep learning (Crooks, 1988). When such learning takes place the learner is actively engaged and integrates learning. The learner understands in relation to his or her own experience and is not just accepting passively ideas or memorising a collection of isolated facts. For example, at Central Park East Secondary School (CPESS), in New York, students' intellectual development is guided by five habits of mind which are fundamental to the goals of the school and the curriculum. These habits of mind involve:

- weighing evidence;
- awareness of varying viewpoints;
- seeing connections and relationships;
- speculating on possibilities;
- assessing value both socially and personally (Darling-Hammond *et al.*, 1995).

These modes of inquiry guide the assessment of student work and appear as criteria incorporated into the assessment instruments for the required graduation portfolio. In the Senior Institute of CPESS students work closely with their advisor and subject teachers on each of their chosen portfolio items. These are revised until student and teachers agree that the work meets the standards of the school. As students prepare work for the portfolio to an appropriate standard they learn about writing, critiquing and revising. Students know the grading criteria so self-evaluation is integral to the process. This is a learning process in itself as, through essential conversations with their advisors and teachers, students are provided with specific concrete feedback that they can use to improve their performance.

The model of formative assessment illustrated here derives from the social constructivist perspective in cognitive psychology that stresses the role of teacher–student interaction in the learning process (Torrance and Pryor, 1998: 15). In referring to the work of Vygotsky and the 'zone of proximal development' (zpd) these authors indicate that it is important not only to state what students have accomplished but to indicate what they are ready to achieve with help. As described:

> The *process* of assessment itself is seen as having an impact on the pupil, as well as the product, the result. ... What we have here, then, is a notion of assessment which looks forward rather than backwards and which envisages teacher–pupil interaction as part of the *assessment* process itself.
>
> (Ibid.)

There is much similarity here with the portfolio processes as outlined in chapter 2.

While the learner's role in formative assessment has been stressed, the teacher has a vital role too. As Black (1998) indicates the teacher has personal knowledge of the student and is in the best position to understand the context of the student's performance. In formative assessment this is important for purposes of validity. Over an extended period of time in the daily work of classroom teaching teachers collect quality, dependable data about students' performances and use this information in their feedback. The intention is for the feedback to impact positively on students' learning. The teacher will be focused on evidence that may indicate an obstacle of misunderstanding with which the student needs help. Validity is vitally important because the essential purpose of formative assessment is transformative, in that there is action based on the feedback towards integration of learning and development in understanding. This type of assessment requires validity in content, construct and consequential aspects.

An important purpose of formative assessment is to identify learning needs; therefore it is criterion-referenced, domain-referenced and student-referenced or ipsative. It is therefore a self-referenced approach where information is used diagnostically in relation to the individual student. Feedback becomes fundamental and needs to be specific to the particular learning needs of the individual student.

Feedback

Feedback is information about how successfully something has been or is being done. Sadler (1989: 120) quotes Ramaprasad's (1983) definition which describes feedback in terms of its effect rather than its informational content: 'information about the gap between the actual level and the reference level of a system parameter which is used to alter the gap in some way'.

The transformative nature of feedback is vital and it is this view of feedback as information that is used to alter the gap that is emphasised by Sadler. He suggests that feedback is not particularly effective if it is recorded simply or if it is too deeply coded (such as a grade) to lead to appropriate action. A grade can divert attention from fundamental judgements and the criteria for making them. In this way a grade can be counterproductive for formative purposes. Sadler suggests that students need more than summary grades if they are to develop expertise intelligently. Hattie and Jaeger (1998: 113) define feedback as the provision of information related to the understanding of the constructions that students have made from the learned or taught information. They (1998: 120) make the important point that feedback that draws attention away from the task and towards the personal attributes can have a negative effect on attitudes and performances.

The quality of feedback is therefore a crucial issue and Sadler (1998: 78) indicates:

> Students should . . . be trained in how to interpret feedback, how to make connections between the feedback and the characteristics of the work they produce, and how they can improve their work in the future. It cannot . . . be assumed that when students are 'given feedback' they will know what to do with it.

Sadler (1998: 78) outlines the phases of feedback development. He explains that originally it derived from stimulus–response theory. Feedback was identified with knowledge of results so that remediation would follow when the response was incorrect and reinforcement was given for the correct response for the intended outcomes of higher motivation and hence higher achievement. The second phase was concerned with praise for effort that would lead to higher self-esteem, more effort, and finally higher achievement. The third phase, the focus of recent research, gives more attention to specific feedback tailored to both the nature of the assessment task and the learner's response to that task. To attain high standards and high achievement the learner needs to appreciate what constitutes high-quality work and understand the required strategies to achieve it.

Feedback to fulfil its transformative function relies on what the teacher does to provide the feedback to the student and what the teacher brings to assessment episodes to make it possible (Sadler, 1998: 79). Sadler describes the typical teacher feedback act as follows. First the teacher focuses on the learner's production. In the development of the portfolio of work, this can be an item of work for inclusion. The teacher judges the work in relation to a background or reference framework to reflect and identify strengths and weaknesses. Sadler stresses that this is a comparative process, though sometimes the point or item of comparison is elusive. The teacher's judgement is made explicit by:

- assigning the learner's work to a class (as in grading);
- mapping the work on to a number line (marking); or
- providing a verbal statement about the quality that incorporates the reasons for the judgement and ways in which some of the weaknesses could be addressed (ibid.).

For this to happen teachers need to have an integrated understanding of the criteria and the standards appropriate to the assessment task. Criteria need to be in a standards-referenced form so that they can be shared with the learner.

Hattie and Jaeger (1998: 111) point out the importance of the interrelationship of assessment, learning and feedback in their model of teaching and learning based on five postulates. These are:

- that achievement is enhanced to the degree that students and teachers set challenging goals relative to the students' present competencies;
- that achievement is enhanced as a function of feedback;
- that achievement is enhanced to the extent that students are trained to receive feedback to verify rather than enhance their sense of efficacy of achievement and to the degree that teachers use reinforcement to help verify rather than enhance students' sense of efficacy;
- that achievement is enhanced to the extent that teachers become more automatic in many of the key teaching competencies, such that they can spend more time providing feedback to students;
- that increases in student learning follow a reconceptualisation of already acquired information as well as the acquisition of new information.

The role of feedback is vital in all of the postulates. Achievement can be enhanced by setting challenging goals relative to the students' existing level of competence. It is goal setting plus feedback that is the most effective. Feedback increases the probability that learning will occur. However, simply providing feedback to students is not enough because it is the ways and manner in which individuals interpret feedback that is the key to developing meaningful learning. Hattie and Jaeger (1998) describe two processes that are used when integrating information. The first of these is 'self-status quo tendencies' which refer to the preservation of concept of self. The second is 'self-testing tendencies' which refer to the seeking of confirmation or disconfirmation about conceptions of self. Teachers need to be aware of individual students' dispositions to receiving feedback information.

The level of expertise of the teacher and his or her 'level of automaticity' determines the extent to which there is feedback to the teacher, and by the teacher to the students. The final postulate conceptualises knowledge as a restructuring process rather than one of accumulation. Assessment in the classroom relates often to knowledge acquisition and 'ignores the other functions of learning such as deep understanding, efficient intuitive use, acquiring multiple flexible strategies, adaptive action control and achievement motivation' (ibid.: 119).

Cognitive processes used by students such as self-regulation and self-monitoring are fundamental to understanding individual constructions and achievement. These become more multidimensional and hierarchical as students develop. Using a portfolio for assessment and learning purposes can inform teachers and students about this reconceptualisation of knowledge. Skills and knowledge are constructed and demonstrated in many different ways. A portfolio approach that incorporates performance assessment encourages diverse modes of presentation and provides teachers with insights into these important cognitive processes. This is because the portfolio is a way of both developing and assessing students' abilities.

Performance assessment

Performance assessment requires the student to construct a response, create a product or demonstrate what they can do and understand. Such assessments can form an integral part of the portfolio of work. Performance assessments according to Baker (1997) have the following characteristics:

- complex thinking;
- open-ended;
- meaningful;
- language dependent;
- time-intensive;
- group or individuals;
- usually scored by judges.

It is important to understand that there are two types of standards that are relevant in a discussion of performance assessments. First, there are content standards that incorporate curriculum aims and subject matter. Second, performance standards that specify content standards into types of performance and the levels of achievement expected. For example, for the performance of a particular form of problem-solving, which expects the use of measurement and scientific knowledge, assessment could be according to the three levels of achievement of excellent, pass or below proficiency.

Performance standards are developmental and incorporate the concept of progress. It is helpful to the learner to understand that the refinement and improvement of outcomes are central to the task and its evaluation. Performance standards allow novices the opportunity to acknowledge and integrate feedback regarding their development.

There are problems associated with performance assessments. Baker (1997) indicates that assessing according to content and performance standards is problematic. Difficulties arise in setting performance standards and in relation to the validity of performance assessments. For example, 'are the standards . . . identified actually predicting the performance of students in subsequent courses' (ibid.: 18)?

With the open-ended nature of performance assessments, teachers need to judge the adequacy of various responses. Baker's research concluded that staff development is important for conducting these assessments because differences in teachers' content understanding impacts on the quality of ratings. Baker found some dramatic effects related to the impact of gaps in teacher knowledge and these have caused problems with the reliability of portfolio assessments. However, reliability appears not to be such a problem when tasks are well structured, teachers have a shared understanding of the scoring criteria that are standards-referenced and consistent assessment procedures are used.

Validity

Black (1998) argues that any assessment instrument does not possess validity in isolation but rather the validity depends on the way in which the result is interpreted. Messick's (1989: 13) notion of validity is apt here.

> Validity is an integrated evaluative judgment of the degree to which empirical evidence and theoretical rationales support the adequacy and appropriateness of inferences and actions based on test scores or other modes of assessment . . .

Validity in this case refers to the evidence available for assessment interpretation and the potential consequences of assessment use.

Validity has been defined as the extent to which an assessment, test or examination does what it was designed to do or measures what it claims to measure. Nuttall (1987: 109) states that all assessments are based on a sample of behaviour or performance in which we are interested. It is from a sample that we generalise to 'the universe of that behaviour'. For example, for a teacher to assess that a student is able to read fluently, a generalisation would have to be made from limited evidence. Nuttall (1987: 110) explains that the 'fidelity of the inference drawn from the responses to the assessment is what is called the validity of the assessment'. The specification of the domain of behaviour in which we are interested is critically important.

In establishing a portfolio system of assessment it is crucial that the domain of behaviour is described. For as Nuttall (1987: 111) suggests '[I]f we cannot define the universe, we can hardly be expected to judge how representative the sample of behaviour we assess actually is. . . . validation is a difficult process . . . and is impossible if we do not have a clear idea of what it is we are trying to assess.'

Nuttall (1987: 115) has indicated that the tasks and conditions that elicit the individual's best performance, and are evident in educational assessment, include:

- tasks that are concrete and within the experience of the individual;
- tasks that are presented clearly;
- tasks that are perceived as relevant to the current concerns of the student;
- conditions that are not unduly threatening, something that is helped by a good relationship between the assessor and the student.

However, improving the tasks and conditions that elicit best performance will not automatically improve validity. Nuttall (1987: 116) stresses that this is best achieved by 'improving the sampling of tasks and the contexts from the universe of interest – and that means defining the universe very much more carefully than we have done in the past'.

Traditionally validity has been defined in terms of type. To illustrate:

- Content validity which describes how well the tasks sample a defined content domain, e.g. does the assessment of the work in the portfolio align with the learning and teaching objectives?
- Construct validity which describes how well results can be interpreted as assessing the test's focal construct, e.g. does the assessment of the work in the portfolio reflect the underlying skill or construct such as verbal reasoning or problem-solving in mathematics?
- Criterion-related validity which describes how well results correlate or predict criterion measures external to the focal assessment (Nitko, 1998: 5).

Validity is now considered a unitary concept when organised around construct validity. A portfolio of work will contain a variety of evidence to demonstrate the skill or underlying construct to be assessed. Construct validity refers to whether the assessment of this evidence adequately measures the underlying skill or construct and supports the inferences and actions based on the assessment. With a collection of evidence the assessor or teacher needs to be aware of the threats to construct validity that have been identified by Messick (1994: 14). These are 'construct underrepresentation' which 'jeopardizes authenticity' because not all the intended criteria are used in the assessment of the portfolio of work and 'construct irrelevant variance' which 'jeopardizes directness' because assessment is too broad, using criteria that were not intended.

Content validity, or whether the assessment of the work in the portfolio aligns with the learning and teaching objectives, and predictive validity, which relates to whether the assessment of the portfolio of work predicts accurately some future performance, are aspects that are important to portfolio assessment. Performance assessments have higher predictive validity than paper-and-pencil tests (Nuttall, 1987: 112).

Nitko (1998) refers to Kane's framework of argument-based validation as useful in validating new assessments. This framework asks us to describe:

- the interpretations we propose to make of the results;
- the reasons why this interpretation is relevant to the use we plan to make of the results; and
- the evidence we have collected that supports the proposed interpretation in the context of the use we plan to make of the results.

Assessments made from a comprehensive and thoughtful process, grounded in a multifaceted body of evidence, are more likely to be valid and lead to continuing improvement (Kimball and Hanley, 1998: 200). There are many types of evidence that can be used in support of the validity argument. This is one reason why educators, such as Moss (1998), argue for an integrative approach for the assessment of a portfolio work. This contrasts with an 'aggregative' approach, grounded in the psychometric paradigm, where scores are assigned by individual assessors to each entry and are combined algorithmically into a composite or profile of scores. Moss (1994: 7) describes the typical psychometric approach to assessment as follows:

- Each performance is scored independently by readers who have no additional knowledge about the student or about the judgements of other readers.
- Inferences about achievement, competence, or growth are based upon composite scores, aggregated from independent observations across readers and performances, and referenced to relevant criteria or norm groups.
- The scores are provided to users with guidelines for interpretation.
- Users are advised to consider scores in the light of other information about the individual, although little guidance is given about how to combine such information to reach a well-warranted conclusion.

The hermeneutic approach to assessment, on the other hand, Moss suggests, involves holistic, integrative interpretations of collected performances that:

- seek to understand the whole in light of its parts;
- privilege readers who are most knowledgeable about the context in which the assessment occurs;
- ground those interpretations not only in textual and contextual evidence available, but also in a rational debate among the community of interpreters.

Hermeneutic philosophy underpins the portfolio assessment approach advocated by Moss (1994: 7). This is because of the holistic and integrative approach to interpretation of human phenomena that seeks to understand the whole in light of its parts. There is a need to repeatedly test interpretations against the available evidence until each of the parts can be accounted for in a coherent interpretation of the whole. Therefore an integrative assessment approach is highly analytic and includes a series of steps involving data reduction and integration. These steps are guided by questions from a detailed assessment framework.

Moss suggests that assessors of a portfolio of work need to take written notes, determine and record relevant evidence, and construct interpretive summaries of the evidence in response to the guiding questions. At each stage the steps of data reduction and integration are recorded for consideration at the next stage. By the time consensus on the overall conclusion is reached assessors have produced a written record of steps in data reduction and integration to which they can return easily. This approach differs from holistic scoring which encourages assessors to form a general impression, informed by a scoring guide or benchmark. This does not involve explicit intermediate analysis in the determination of the holistic score.

Standards

A standard as defined by Cresswell (1996: 13) is 'the value accorded to students' work by judges accepted by all interested parties as competent to make such judgements'. Standards are statements that indicate the different levels of quality of performance. If assessment is to be entirely portfolio-based for summative purposes then there is a need for standards to be developed and disseminated to ensure reliability and comparability across institutions.

This is particularly true for high-stakes assessment. However, as indicated by Wolf (1998) from the experience of the National Council for Vocational Qualifications (NCVQ) in England and Wales, written descriptors cannot be written so tightly that they can be applied reliably by multiple assessors to various assessment situations.

Wolf (1998) points out the essential role of professional judgement and of contact among professional communities in creating and maintaining standards. The implications for teachers and lecturers are the need for content expertise so they can develop criteria and know what to expect of students at various levels. Teachers need to be able to use performance criteria to recognise standards of performance to guide students in the selection of the work for the portfolio such that it is representative of performance. This implies the need for teachers to meet regularly to discuss work for moderation purposes. Such professional collaboration would help to prevent what Cresswell (1996) refers to as the repeated failure of attempts to implement standards that are based upon the 'mechanical application' of explicit criteria.

Mabry (1999) has indicated that standards can be classified into three types; content, performance and delivery, equity or opportunity standards. Content standards indicate intended learning outcomes or what should be taught. They are more general than performance standards, which consist of concrete examples or explicit definitions of what students must know and do to demonstrate proficiency. Delivery, equity or opportunity standards incorporate explicit criteria for assessing the adequacy of resources provided to students. Mabry (1999: 63) warns: 'there has been little critical consideration as to whether we *should* have standards-based assessment, whether we *should* expect kids to learn the same things to a particular level of proficiency'.

Reliability

Reliability refers to 'the accuracy with which an assessment measures the skill or attainment it is designed to measure' (Gipps, 1994: vii). The essential reliability question is: would the assessment of a portfolio of work result in the same or similar assessment on two occasions if assessed by two assessors? This assessment concept is more relevant for portfolios used for summative purposes and is less of a concern for formative assessment. Gipps (1994) summarises the definition of reliability by indicating that it relates to consistency of student performance and consistency in assessing that performance: replicability and comparability.

Criterion-referenced assessed work focuses on the work of the individual rather than the comparison with other students and the differences among individuals. Therefore traditional reliability tests are not appropriate. What does need to be considered in portfolio assessment, which incorporates performance assessment, is the consistency of approach to the assessment task as well as consistency of standards in assessment. Tasks need to be administered consistently and therefore guidelines and professional development are needed. The consistency of standards relates to ensuring that different assessors interpret the assessment criteria in the same way. Assessment criteria can be open to different interpretations and therefore for reliability purposes it is necessary for moderation to occur. The aim of moderation is to achieve consistency in assessment for the enhancement of quality.

Group moderation is needed when implementing a portfolio approach to assessment. Groups of lecturers or teachers need to discuss the portfolios of work in relation to their understanding of the criteria and standards used for assessment. Initial meetings would need to occur within the institution or school where the system was being implemented. Meetings across schools or institutions could then follow and would help improve consistency of judgements of portfolio contents at the system level.

To ensure consistent marking and to improve the process of judging the portfolio contents, Forster and Masters (1996: 43) refer to the work of Herman who recommends the following to ensure reliability of rating procedures:

- documented, field-tested scoring guides;
- clear, concrete criteria;
- annotated examples of all score points;
- ample practice and feedback for raters;
- multiple raters with demonstrated agreement prior to scoring;
- periodic reliability checks throughout;
- retraining where necessary; and
- arrangements for collection of suitable reliability data.

Summative assessment

Summative assessment implies an overview of past performance. In a portfolio of work this is an accumulation of evidence over a specified period of time. The purpose of summative assessment is to determine the extent to which the student's work has met given target criteria (Wiliam and Black, 1996). Transfer between different stages of schooling, between different institutions and between different teachers requires assessment information to be structured. Black (1998) has indicated that the following criteria need to be addressed:

- The assessment information has to be adequately detailed. Grades are insufficient detail, and a profile that shows variations in this grade between such aspects as practical investigative work, factual knowledge, numerical problem-solving is more useful.
- Common criteria are needed for grading so that the teachers involved in the assessment are focused on the same aspects of learning, such as structure of argument, coherence of expression.
- There should be a shared procedure for determining standards of grading so that teachers use the same criteria and have the same standards for interpreting them.

There are several approaches that can be adopted in assessing a portfolio of work for summative purposes. For example, the assessment may take a holistic approach or one that is analytic. With the latter approach the different aspects of the portfolio of work are assessed separately and judgements about the quality of the parts are aggregated to obtain a total grade. Adding or averaging the assessments of each of the included pieces of work of the portfolio is often the way that the final grade is determined. The former approach is holistic and involves the assessment of the whole portfolio rather than assessment of each individual inclusion. The focus is on the overall quality with attention to how the individual pieces of work contribute to the whole. Mabry (1999: 63) has indicated that the analytic approach is more likely to be adopted when the criteria are pre-specified as each criterion directs attention to a specific aspect of the work. She suggests (ibid.: 64) that holistic assessment can be guided by general questions which require attention 'to both the overall quality of the [portfolio of] work and to the specific contributing aspects'. In this way Mabry explains that the assessor evaluates the student's performance on the basis of what the student has done rather than on prior expectations that may not necessarily align with the student's performance.

In Kentucky, writing portfolios form a component of a more comprehensive, complex assessment system. These portfolios are collections of a student's best work developed throughout the school year. For example, the work in a grade-4 writing portfolio presented for summative assessment comprises:

- a personal narrative;
- a poem, play or piece of fiction;
- one informative or persuasive piece;
- one piece from any subject area other than English and language arts;
- a best piece; and

- a letter to the reviewer about the best piece and the student's growth as a writer.

The axiological criteria or dimensions for assessment include:

- purpose and approach;
- idea development;
- organisation;
- sentences;
- wording; and
- surface features.

Assessors rate the entire portfolio according to the standards that are described at four levels of performance: novice, apprentice, proficient and distinguished – as in Figure 3.8. The assessors provide a single grade for the entire portfolio based on best fit rather than meeting all criteria.

Holistic assessment of the portfolio for summative purposes

Using a portfolio for assessment purposes has been described as an 'expansionist' assessment technique (Mabry, 1999). This is because of the amount and variety of evidence submitted in a portfolio of work, which serves as a data base of student performance for assessment of achievement. Mabry (1999: 79) has indicated that this form of assessment is in contrast to more reductionist strategies such as 'standardised norm-referenced multiple choice achievement testing where indications of achievement are reduced to a score'.

The task of assessing expansionist formats, like the portfolio of work, differs from assessing more reductionist techniques. This is because the portfolio consists of multiple entries and requires several essential processes that are not necessary when assessing a single text such as a standardised achievement test, essay or assignment (Heller *et al.*, 1998). When preparing teachers or assessors for the assessment of portfolios of work these processes should be made explicit. It needs to be remembered, however, that the different purposes for the development of a portfolio will determine the particular assessment processes adopted. When assessing portfolios holistically, individual entries in the portfolio are not rated separately from the collection as a whole.

Heller *et al.* (1998), in their study of raters' or assessors' reasoning during the assessment of standards-based, non-prescriptive portfolios,[1] developed a model that provides insights into the component processes involved in the holistic assessment of this type of portfolio. Students were not required to include particular kinds of work or standardised pieces in their portfolios, unlike the personal studies folio of work for candidates studying Higher Grade English in Scotland. They were able to select work that they believed demonstrated their performance with respect to the 'particular assessment dimensions'. The portfolios were assessed holistically according to these standards. Individual inclusions were not intended to be assessed

Figure 3.8 Extract from Kentucky Department of Education KIRIS Writing Portfolio Assessment, grade 4 assessment training book

Kentucky writing assessment (holistic scoring guide)	
4	• Establishes a purpose and maintains clear focus, strong awareness of audience; evidence of distinct voice • Depth and complexity of ideas supported by rich, engaging and/or pertinent details • Careful and/or subtle organisation • Variety in sentence structure and length enhances effect • Precise and/or rich language • Control of spelling, punctuation and capitalisation
3	• Focused on a purpose; communicates with an audience; evidence of voice and/or subtle tone • Depth of idea development supported by elaborated, relevant details • Logical, coherent organisation • Controlled and varied sentence structure • Acceptable, effective language • Few errors in spelling, punctuation and capitalisation relative to length or complexity
2	• Some evidence of communicating with an audience for a specific purpose: some lapses in focus • Unelaborated idea development; unelaborated and/or repetitious details • Simplistic and/or awkward sentence structure • Simplistic and/or imprecise language • Some errors in spelling, punctuation, and capitalisation that do not interfere with communication
1	• Limited awareness of audience and/or purpose • Minimal idea development; limited and/or unrelated details • Random and/or weak organisation • Incorrect and/or ineffective sentence structure • Incorrect and/or ineffective language • Errors in spelling, punctuation and capitalisation are disproportionate to length and complexity

Source: Kentucky Department of Education, Frankfort, Kentucky 40601 (used with permission).

independently from the collection as a whole. It is in this context that these authors were able to identify three component processes that included:

• the assessment of individual entries in the portfolio one at a time;
• assessing across texts in the portfolio; and
• evaluating the importance of evidence.

These processes differ to the assessment of a single work because assessors engage in iterative and cyclical processing sequences. To illustrate, in assessing the standards-referenced, non-prescriptive portfolio of work the assessors had to 'read and evaluate (but not rate) individual texts repeatedly in the course of evaluating a single portfolio' (ibid.: 9). Assessors in this context also described and evaluated performance by reasoning across evidence in the individual texts included in the portfolio of work. The non-prescriptive nature of this portfolio also required assessors to evaluate the relevance and validity of entries to determine whether they could be considered as credible evidence. This process is also not necessary when assessing more reductionist formats such as a single essay or text. It was found that assessors cycle repeatedly through these component processes of portfolio assessment. Heller *et al.* (1998: 9) conclude that: 'Because there are more component processes involved in rating portfolios than essays, these iterations could generate many variations in reasoning, but the variations would not necessarily represent threats to validity.'

To summarise, assessors did not conduct these processes in a linear fashion; rather they cycled among component processes and among subprocesses. They began by describing and evaluating the qualities of performance across the entries while reading through the portfolio contents for the first time; then they alternated between evaluating individual entries, evaluating part or all of the collection and articulating possible ratings, before finally reaching a decision. There was great variation in the sequencing of processes.

This general process model can be used as a framework to conceptualise assessor reasoning and to evaluate whether assessor variations in their use of the processes of the model threaten the validity of the final assessment. The threats to validity that were identified included:

- omission of essential processes, assessment of portfolios without using important criteria;
- the addition of inappropriate processes or use of extraneous criteria;
- the execution of the processes in a sequence that adversely influences the meaning of the final assessment.

For example, an assessor may not evaluate across the range of texts included in the portfolio but base the final assessment on a judgement of selected inclusions such as the first and last pieces of work incorporated into the portfolio of work. Heller *et al.* (1998) indicate that the resulting assessment would differ in meaning from one that was based on an assessment of the collection of texts in the portfolio.

Major threats to validity and reliability occurred when assessors omitted the use of important criteria provided. This is an example of 'construct underrepresentation' (Messick, 1995) because the failure to use all intended criteria in the assessment of the portfolio of work suggests that the final assessment is not based on a consideration of all important dimensions of the construct. A variation of this threat to validity is when the assessor applies an 'idiosyncratic weighting of criteria' and the example given by Heller *et al.* (1998: 11) is when 'some aspects of performance do not receive sufficient evaluative attention'. These authors also found incidences of 'construct-irrelevant variance' (Messick, 1995) or instances when assessment was too broad. This occurred when assessors used irrelevant or idiosyncratic criteria that were not intended or included in the assessment guidelines.

With a database of student achievement that includes multiple entries, the assessment of the portfolio becomes more complex. It is expected that multiple, underlying constructs will be assessed from the complete portfolio of work, not from a single text or inclusion. Assessors, as is evident from the study conducted by Heller *et al.* (1998), vary in how they go about assessing the contents, in their application of criteria and the way they evaluate the credibility of evidence in and across the various inclusions of the portfolio. Such variations can influence the constructs being assessed, and the greater the variations among assessors the more likely the assessors will disagree in their final assessments. In the assessment of more expansionist forms of assessment, such as the portfolio, it is clear that there will be threats to validity. This has important implications for the design, development and implementation of such assessment systems. Assessors will require assessment guides and professional development in the processes, procedures and concepts involved in assessing a portfolio of work.

Summary

- Knowledge of assessment, understanding of the relationship of assessment and curriculum and recognition of the importance of assessment for learning are essential to use portfolios for assessment and learning profitably.
- Each type of portfolio requires an assessment procedure that fits its particular purpose.
- Developmental assessment (that incorporates progress maps and developmental continua) and criterion referencing are important to consider at the outset of the portfolio design.
- Formative assessment, feedback, performance assessment and validity (content, construct and consequential aspects) are important assessment concepts during the development phase of a portfolio of work.
- When a portfolio is submitted for final assessment and grading purposes, reliability, standards and summative assessment are particularly relevant.
- The processes involved in assessing the portfolio holistically, for summative assessment purposes, are unique to the procedure of assessing multiple entries such as those included in a portfolio of work and differ from evaluating a single test, assignment or text.

4   Problems and pitfalls

In this chapter, the problems and pitfalls experienced in the development and implementation of different portfolio assessment systems in varying contexts will be considered. Portfolio use is in its infancy, and problems have emerged, however much the use of a portfolio for learning and assessment purposes, as has been argued, has to offer. There exists the need to consider how assessment systems can accommodate portfolios as a central component.

Mabry (1999: 23) has suggested:

> Too often, assessment reflects confusion, mismatching purposes to paradigms or techniques. Confusion in assessment policy typically produces systems that unintentionally limit the benefits of a given approach and that fail to accomplish fully the original assessment purpose. If we understand the differences in assessment approaches, we are in a better position to develop coherent assessment systems and to co-ordinate assessment with teaching and learning.

The implementation of intended learning outcomes of a portfolio system can be hindered if the view of assessment does not accept that portfolio pegagogy is pivotal.

From an analysis of the research and literature related to the use of portfolios for assessment it is evident that most attempts to design, develop and implement a portfolio assessment system have encountered problems. These can result from unhelpful policy decisions, conceptual confusions or various forms of practical or technical problems. Dwyer (1998) has also argued that psychological and social barriers inhibit the realisation of assessment for learning. This chapter will deal with each in turn.

Policy decisions

To develop more coherent assessment systems, both curriculum and pedagogy need to align with the purposes and paradigms of educational assessment. This requires an analysis of educational assessment paradigms, as well as the underpinning theories of learning and curriculum design. Such analysis helps to identify appropriate pedagogic practices that support the implementation of new assessment systems.

In emphasising the role of assessment in a learning culture, Shepard (2000) has identified the power of 'enduring and hidden beliefs'. She has developed a historical framework that has its key tenets: social efficiency curriculum, behaviourist learning theories and 'scientific measurement'. She contrasts this with a social-constructivist conceptual framework that combines key ideas from cognitive, constructivist, and socio-cultural theories to illustrate how assessment practices need to change to be consistent with and support social-constructivist pedagogy. The use of portfolios for assessment requires this change. Shepard argues that any attempt to change classroom assessment so that it is integrated into the teaching and learning process will require an understanding and analysis of the power of traditional paradigms and historical beliefs. Reference is made to Thorndike, the originator of associationist learning theory and the father of scientific measurement. His influence led to the dominance of recall and multiple-choice-type tests which matched what it was considered important to learn. Curriculum was seen in terms of these types of items and formats and resulted in a particular and outdated conception of subject matter. She suggests that the dominance of objective tests in classroom practice influenced not only the subject matter of knowledge but also the nature of evidence and principles of fairness. In demonstrating the power of such traditional beliefs Shepard refers to an assessment project where it was discovered that teachers believed it was necessary to keep assessment 'separate from instruction' to maintain the 'objectivity' of assessment practices (Shepard, 2000). This was despite the enthusiasm for developing alternatives to standardised tests. Teachers' beliefs demonstrated their adherence to traditional principles of scientific measurement. The implications are that teachers, especially pre-service teachers, need to understand constructivist assessments, conduct such practices with confidence and value them as alternatives to examination driven systems. 'Teachers . . . need help in learning to use assessment in new ways' (ibid.: 22).

The observation that assessment is often conceived as separate from teaching in both time and purpose (Shepard, 2000) appears in the research of Dwyer (1998). She found that many teachers did not view assessment as integral to their teaching, involving 'an analytical process of collecting evidence about student learning' (ibid.: 134). Teachers did not see their own collection of evidence about student achievement as 'assessment'; rather they viewed assessment as imposed from external agencies and therefore the responsibility of others (Dwyer, 1994). In the research she conducted she found that pre-service teachers experienced difficulty in aligning curriculum aims and assessment to the extent that the assessments given to their students were often unrelated to their teaching and learning goals. Consequently their assessments did not provide the necessary formative or summative evidence about the students' learning. Another related issue that emerged from her work was the way in which teachers conceptualised curricula. The notion of 'covering' the curriculum dominated some teachers' thinking to the exclusion of any attention to the structure of the body of knowledge or content being taught. She concluded that '[u]nderstanding the interrelation-ships of key concepts and other aspects of curriculum structure is a necessary prerequisite to the effective use of assessment evidence to understand learning progress for individuals . . . but it is often not reflected in classroom assessment' (ibid.: 134).

Mabry (1999) has also argued that many of the problems associated with new forms of assessment such as portfolios stem from a mismatch of purpose to paradigm or technique. She discusses psychometric, contextual and personalised paradigms in the context of assessment. She illustrates how in the psychometric paradigm the key to assessment of student achievement is comparison: 'a student's performance is compared to a predetermined standard or cut-score or to the performances of other test takers' (Mabry, 1999: 24). Further characteristics of this paradigm include: standard test content, standardised administration, objective items and formats, use of machine scoring, no self-evaluation and summative reporting and use of results (ibid.).

In the contextual paradigm there is a focus on the curricula students actually experience and what they have learned without comparison to predetermined criteria and standards. Here the essential characteristics as identified by Mabry include: curriculum-sensitive test content, common classroom settings, both objective and subjective assessment items, teacher assessment, use of self-evaluation and both formative and summative forms of assessment.

The personalised paradigm incorporates self-evaluation. This is because of the importance of ' self-knowledge as a basis for all understanding and the importance of metacognitive self-monitoring' (ibid.: 30). The key characteristics of this paradigm include: student-sensitive test content, time and setting of assessments varying according to the student, use of subjective items with some selection by the student, and teacher-assessed work or other assessed work. Self-evaluation is essential and formative use of results may also include summative assessments (ibid.: 24).

Mabry (1999) contends that new assessment systems that are implemented within an old and inappropriate paradigm will be limited in effect because of the tensions and internal conflicts that will inevitably emerge. To illustrate this, she refers to the development of a portfolio of work or performance tasks that yield individual information and evidence of achievement that is reduced to a few scores.

In this chapter further examples of the power of historical beliefs and the mismatch of policy purposes and paradigms have been drawn from the United States, England, Wales and Northern Ireland. The mismatch of policy purposes to assessment paradigms is illustrated clearly by the problems that have emerged in the implementation of large-scale portfolio assessment programmes. The use of portfolios in Vermont and Kentucky in the United States will be described first. Some brief examples of portfolio programmes at further education, secondary and primary levels in England, Wales and Northern Ireland will then be illustrated. An analysis of the problems that have emerged in varying contexts will illustrate the complexity of the issues involved.

United States: Vermont and Kentucky

In the United States, Koretz (1998) has evaluated the performance data produced by large-scale portfolio assessment programmes such as those in Vermont and

Kentucky. He concludes that in the United States the use of portfolios for large-scale external assessment is problematic given its current stage of development. Until recently Vermont was the only state in the US that had portfolio assessment as the core of its state-wide large-scale assessment programme. Koretz (1998) explains that the portfolio component has since been reduced due to new state policies. Previously students were required to develop portfolios of work in mathematics and writing for one year. In mathematics, teacher and student selected five to seven pieces of work from the working portfolio. For assessment purposes seven dimensions of performance were identified (four pertaining to problem-solving and three to communication) and a four-level scale was set for each. In writing, students were required to submit a portfolio of work consisting of their 'best piece' and several others of specified types. Five dimensions for assessment were specified (purpose, organisation, details, voice/tone, and usage/mechanics/grammar) and a four-level scale was set for each dimension. Teachers who had not taught the students assessed the portfolios for state-reporting purposes.

In Kentucky, unlike Vermont, the use of portfolios for assessment purposes was a modest component embedded in a comprehensive, complex assessment system. However, the writing portfolios were used for accountability purposes and were a significant but not dominant component of the changing assessment programme. In mathematics the portfolio of work was initially used for developmental purposes in the first cycle; then for accountability reasons in the second biennial cycle, only to be removed again in the third. The writing portfolio was intended to be the foundation on which the writing programme was based, and it was assessed in grades 4, 8 and 12. For example, in grade 4, from a working portfolio of one year's work an assessment portfolio comprising six pieces was developed. The work selected for inclusion comprised: a personal narrative; a poem, play or piece of fiction; one informative or persuasive piece; one piece from any subject area other than English and language arts; a best piece and a letter to the reviewer about the best piece and the student's growth as a writer (Koretz, 1998: 317). Six dimensions (purpose and approach, idea development, organisation, sentences, wording and surface features) were used. However, unlike in Vermont, assessors did not grade on the individual dimensions and each piece of work was not assessed on each dimension. Assessors were provided with assessment criteria that described in general terms the dimension at four levels of performance: novice; apprentice; proficient and distinguished. The assessors provided a single grade for the entire portfolio.

An example of how policy can impact on the intended use of portfolios is illustrated by the research of Callahan (1997). This study in a high school in Kentucky looked at the implementation of writing portfolios in grades 4, 8 and 12. While the original intention was that the writing portfolio would be both for improvement of writing and for professional development and accountability purposes, the reality was that the accountability purpose was the one stressed by the Kentucky Department of Education. Callahan found that the teachers felt their competence was being assessed and as a result they were under pressure to produce good portfolio scores rather than consider the pedagogical benefits of portfolio assessment per se. The assessment portfolios did promote change in both the amount and kind of writing produced and the criteria used to assess student writing but there was not much change in the way student writing was understood or taught.

The focus on the use of the writing portfolio for teacher accountability purposes inhibited the development of a 'portfolio pedagogy' (ibid.) and thus the intended learning for both student and teacher. To change the format of the assessment to portfolios and then to use them for teacher accountability purposes illustrates the mismatch of purposes to assessment paradigms and the confusion in assessment policy. Teachers need to engage in professional development that will support the integration of the assessment practice into the curriculum and their teaching practice, and the policy context needs to be supportive of such change.

In both Vermont and Kentucky where portfolios have been used for large-scale assessment purposes, changes to the original intention have occurred due to state policies. The tensions that emerge because the assessment system is implemented within a traditional paradigm have limited the effect of the portfolio on promoting intended learning outcomes. The mismatch of policy purposes and paradigms is apparent.

England, Wales and Northern Ireland: NVQs, GNVQs and RoAs

Portfolios are used for high-stakes assessment and certification purposes in England, Wales and Northern Ireland in the National Vocational Qualifications (NVQs) and General National Vocational Qualifications (GNVQs) programmes. NVQs and GNVQs are the responsibility of the Qualifications and Curriculum Authority (QCA). NVQs are job-specific while GNVQs are designed to develop knowledge, skills and understandings in broad vocational areas. Wolf (1998) suggests that the use of portfolios in these programmes is underpinned by a belief in teaching and learning approaches that facilitate students' independence and initiative. The implications for pedagogy are that teachers need to provide students with the opportunities to develop important metacognitive skills that will increase self-awareness of processes to help them plan, monitor, organise and control their own learning. Students build up a portfolio of evidence to demonstrate that they have completed each task. Such evidence can include written reports on activities, photographs, videos or recordings of practical work.

The 1990s reform of qualification structures in England, Wales and Northern Ireland saw the emergence of GNVQ – a unit based qualification available at levels 1–3 (Foundation, Intermediate and Advanced). This is an alternative to GCSE/ GCE qualification and is mainly taken by sixteen- to nineteen-year-old students in full-time education. The outcomes can be either a place in further/higher education or a significant component in a CV on entry to employment, so in both cases it can be seen as a form of high-stakes assessment.

The assessment process for both NVQs and GNVQs requires the development of a portfolio of work. An NVQ, which is specifically a vocational award, requires the assessment of outcomes specified according to occupational standards. Evidence is collected over time, especially in the workplace, to ensure validity and credibility with employers. It is also possible to claim credit for work completed in the past. In their evaluation of NVQ assessment Eraut *et al.* (1996) concluded that the necessity to record evidence for assessment and quality assurance purposes helps to explain the adoption of portfolios. Quality assurance requires external verification of work for confirmation of the award. It is this procedure that is the catalyst for the compilation of the portfolio of work. Consequently,

> the portfolio [is] a pile of paper which may or may not fit into one receptacle. Some of the paper will be the candidate's work; some of it will consist of assessment forms (logbooks) . . . and there may be artwork, or videos, or other additional evidence attached. What almost all portfolios have in common is size.
>
> (Wolf, 1998: 420)

The dominant purpose of the portfolio is to record evidence for quality assurance purposes and to verify work for confirmation of the award. The emphasis is on the verification of the work. Tensions emerge when the essential processes required in developing the portfolio – self-evaluation, substantive dialogue about the work and critical reflection – are undervalued. Portfolio pedagogy is limited because of the demands to prove rather than to improve learning. The opportunity for metacognitive development is lost.

The GNVQ has undergone continuous modification since its inception. The original GNVQ emphasised students taking responsibility for their own learning, using their own local experience and developing personal skills. The model was based on the competency model used in the National Vocational Qualifications. In the very earliest draft form of the GNVQ there were no tests or grading, other than pass/fail. As in the case of the NVQs the assessment process required the candidate to present evidence that each outcome had been achieved. Wolf (1998) explains that portfolios for GNVQs are used for selection purposes and therefore must be credible. Due to a ministerial directive GNVQs were required to include an element of external examinations. Basic factual material was tested by external simple, multiple-choice mastery tests. They contained 25–30 items at Foundation and 30–40 items at Intermediate and Advanced and required a pass mark of 70 per cent. Their effectiveness was limited by not being pre-tested and by not contributing to grading beyond pass/fail (Stobart, 2001). However, the assessment system developed for GNVQs still included portfolio assessment as a major component and this formed the 'the sole basis for grading decisions' (Wolf, 1998: 422). Grading criteria for the GNVQ award included:

- the ability to plan one's work;
- the ability to seek and handle information;
- the ability to evaluate approaches, outcomes and alternatives; and
- mastery of content was added later.

These four dimensions were equally weighted and applied to the overall portfolio. There were three levels of performance: pass, merit and distinction. Guidance to tutors in the form of exemplar work at the three levels of performance and annotated and analysed excerpts from student work were published to help teachers in the assessment of GNVQ portfolios.

The four grading themes (planning, information-seeking and handling, evaluation and quality of outcomes) were subdivided and contained complex criteria. Teachers complained that the assessment requirements were difficult and demanded they check whether students had met all their performance and grading criteria. Figure 4.1 illustrates the 1995 specifications for the Unit 1: Business organisations and employment at Intermediate level. In 1995 the Capey Review (NCVQ, 1995) of the assessment of GNVQ found that such a detailed system of assessment and the complex grading criteria were unmanageable and burdensome for teachers (Stobart, 2001). The recommendations have increased external components to improve reliability. The revised GNVQ at advanced level incorporates tougher tests, tighter rules on re-sits, separate grading of each unit, external assessment only of one-third of the units and a final grade based on performance in every unit rather than 'one third of the evidence' as was the case in 2000. These changes are specifically designed to introduce greater rigour and ensure comparability with A Level. Advanced Level GNVQs are now known as 'vocational A Levels'. It is planned that from September 2002 Foundation, Intermediate and Part One GNVQs will be restructured and known as vocational GCSEs.[1]

It is suggested that GNVQs will continue to be substantially different from A levels in the methods of study and assessment. GNVQ courses are designed to be more work-related and to emphasise practical research. Two-thirds of the work is internally marked, compared with about 30 per cent for A Levels.

The attempt to achieve parity with the A Level qualification demonstrates the power of traditional paradigms and historical beliefs. A central purpose of the GNVQ portfolio is to promote students' responsibility for their own learning, use of their own local experience and development of personal skills. This requires assessment practices aligned to contextual or personalised paradigms and a portfolio pedagogy. However, the recent policy changes to GNVQ assessment shift the emphasis to tests and external assessments derived from a psychometric paradigm. The benefits of the portfolio for student learning and assessment are likely to be limited by this reorganisation in emphasis.

The National Record of Achievement was introduced in schools in England, Wales and Scotland during 1991. In Northern Ireland a separate pilot project was established resulting in the National Record of Achievement being introduced in 1992. This initiative, according to Broadfoot (1998a), was about reporting achievement and improving student motivation and learning. The emphasis was on recording achievement in addition to assessing performance. The value of having a means to communicate a student's academic achievements, skills, social and personal qualities and experiences to further education institutions, admission tutors and employers was recognised. This 'portfolio' was to be compiled jointly by students and their teacher. The original intention was that the 'portfolio' would be used both as a planning tool and a record of achievements but the extent to which this has happened has been variable. The National Record of Achievement

Figure 4.1 1995 Specifications Unit 1: Business Organisations and Employment (Intermediate)

Element 1.1: Explain the purposes and types of business organisations

PERFORMANCE CRITERIA
A student must:
1. describe **developments** in **industrial sectors**
2. explain the **purposes** of **business organisations**
3. explain the **differences** between **types of business ownership**
4. explain the **operation** of one business organisation

RANGE
Developments: recent, past, present, likely future; growth of the sector, decrease of the sector; typical activities in the sector
Industrial sectors: primary, secondary, tertiary
Purposes: profit, market share, customer service, public service, charitable
Business organisations: private sector, public sector; large, medium, small
Differences: type of liability (limited, unlimited), use of profit (owners, shareholders, government)
Types of business ownership: sole trader, partnership, private limited company (Ltd), public limited company (plc), franchise, cooperative, state-owned
Operation: location; product (goods, services); links with other businesses; purpose; type of ownership

EVIDENCE INDICATORS
A summary which describes developments in the primary, secondary and tertiary sectors; focusing on present growth or decrease in each sector and typical activities in the sectors.

Seven examples of different business organisations which have different types of ownership. For each example a summary which explains the purposes and differences between types of business organisation. The seven business organisations should include at least one public sector organisation and small, medium and large private sector organisations.

Source: NCVQ (1995).

A report which focuses on one local or national business organisation, explaining its location, product, purpose, type of ownership and its links with other businesses.

AMPLIFICATION
Developments (PC1) the main focus of study should be on the present developments with just a brief overview of the recent past and some suggestions for what may happen in the near future.
Profit (PC2 range and PC3) students should understand that in making profit businesses create wealth. They should also understand the basic distribution of profits, including the argument for retaining profits in business.
Public service (PC2 range) students should understand that public service organisations exist to meet the needs of the public as identified by a government.
Differences between types of business ownership (PC3) students should be able to recognise and explain the differences in terms of the number and status of the owner or owners, and should be able to describe who controls the business organisation. They should also understand that different types of business will access different sources of finance.
Links with other businesses (PC4 range) refers to regular routine contacts with suppliers and customers.

GUIDANCE
For this element students need access to background information about business. This information could vary from area to area, and staff should adapt learning programmes to meet local circumstances. For example, descriptions of developments in industrial sectors might focus on the decline of mining or the growth of franchising. The report on one business organisation may look at the organisation in the primary, secondary or tertiary business sector.
Through studying the differences between types of ownership, students should understand that businesses have legal responsibilities in terms of liability and other responsibilities, notably decisions about profit distribution taken by the owners or directors of the business.

Review (1997: 7) concluded: 'Beyond school the current National Record of Achievement is used much less frequently. As a document for helping lifelong learning, career planning and employees' prospects across the United Kingdom economy, it has failed.' It is not surprising that this conclusion has been reached given the dual aims of the Record of Achievement (RoA). It was to fulfil both the formative function of helping pupils focus on their learning needs and also to plan for their development. At the same time it was intended that the RoA would also fulfil a summative purpose in providing a record of pupil achievement across the national curriculum on nationally designated targets (Broadfoot, 1998a). The tension exists because the education system values formal summative examinations and hence assessment that measures learning over the pedagogical and learning purpose of 'portfolios'.

Conceptual confusion

In this section examples of conceptual confusion are illustrated when those who are responsible for the implementation of portfolio systems sometimes fail to understand their nature and the importance of associated pedagogical changes. When the portfolios are implemented the prevailing understanding of the nature and purpose of assessment sometimes militates against their success. The context in which the portfolios are used can also distort the portfolio process and associated benefits.

There is no agreement about the most effective method for portfolio implementation. To a large extent the implementation strategy is governed by the intended purpose of the portfolio and the policy context. For example, the portfolio was introduced as part of the curriculum in Kentucky where it is the foundation on which the writing programme is based. In England and Wales portfolios were intended for the General National Vocational Qualification as a system of progress monitoring and personal tutoring but also to demonstrate understanding and skills.

The use of assessment for purposes of enhancing learning and for empowering learners is valid. However, attitudes of students and teachers are difficult to change in institutions and contexts where traditional conceptions of assessment use, such as for measuring learning, dominate. Broadfoot (1998a: 466) characterises the current context in England and Wales as follows:

- a national programme of testing of pupil attainment at ages seven, eleven and fourteen (Key Stages 1, 2 and 3);
- major summative assessment of all pupils at age sixteen (General Certificate of Secondary Education, GCSE);
- A-Level examinations at age eighteen;
- publication of test and examination results in the form of league tables comparing the performance of schools;
- school inspections;
- decline in the use of coursework in external examinations; and
- the requirement for schools to set targets and benchmarks to determine their value-added component.

Thus she argues that the prevailing assessment culture is one of measurement rather than of support for pedagogy and learning functions. Broadfoot's analysis helps to explain why the use of portfolios or Records of Achievement (RoA) has encountered difficulties. Broadfoot and Pollard (1997: 45) draw on contemporary research evidence and conclude that:

> the combined effect of recent policy changes in assessment has been to reinforce traditionalist conceptions of teaching and learning which are associated with a greater instrumentalism on the part of pupils . . . rather than acquiring life-long learning skills and attitudes, the effect of recent reforms has been to make pupils more dependent on the teacher and less ready and able to engage in 'deep' learning.

Broadfoot (1996) suggests that students see assessment as defining what is important, how they allocate their time and how they see themselves as learners. McDowell and Sambell (1999) studied students' perspectives on their experiences of some of the newer 'alternative' forms of assessment in higher education in England. These included a series of reflective tasks presented in a portfolio of written responses together with an oral presentation. They found that assessment influences how students use their time and engage in tasks that they perceive as necessary to meet the requirements. Students base their decisions about where to concentrate their efforts in relation to the nature of the learning and studying promoted by the assessment requirement and also to whether these assessment requirements motivate them to learn. For example, some students felt that some assessment requires 'poor' learning: 'You shallow learn for an exam, but you don't *know* the stuff. It's poor learning, which you quickly forget' (ibid.: 116). In many cases these researchers found that students seemed to agree that the nature of assessment tasks could really help them to learn: 'I found [by the end of the academic year] that you always knew the subject you'd done your [oral] presentation on really well' (ibid.). Biggs (1996) has also reported research evidence that demonstrates students will analyse an assessment system to develop strategies that will enable them to score high grades efficiently. This is why the assessment system and policy context need to align with intentions of promoting learning and teaching.

Snyder *et al.* (1998) highlight the inherent tension between assessment for support and assessment for high-stakes decision making. This concern is discussed in the context of the use of portfolios in the University of California, Santa Barbara (UCSB), teacher education programmes. Of the two portfolios considered, the first is a Masters in education (M.Ed.) portfolio that has been designed and implemented to encourage reflection on individual teaching practice to help focus on the developmental processes in teaching experience for learning purposes. The second is a credential portfolio developed with externally defined standards in mind and tends to be a collection of artefacts that provide evidence of the student's work. The candidate is required to 'prove' competence against state-defined standards. For these authors a major concern is the notion of 'proving competence' to the neglect of using the portfolio as an opportunity to record growth through 'honest reflections on struggles and inevitable failures common to the learning process' (ibid.: 124). The issue that emerges is that the use of portfolios for summative purposes can potentially distort their use as a learning strategy and a process which allows the student to make her or his practice explicit for reflection and inquiry purposes. The intention in Santa Barbara was clearly to encourage students in the critical analysis and critique of their own practice to improve and develop professional knowledge, skills and dispositions. The ability to reflect on work was possible because the process for both portfolios required the documentation of thought and practice developmentally over time. To make their learning explicit students were required to collect, select and reflect on evidence of how they were thinking and what they were doing at stages throughout the preparation year.

To address the tension between assessment for support and assessment for summative purposes, changes have been made. For the purpose of providing credentials, the California Standards for the Teaching Profession, grounded in teacher development, have been adopted as they are more useful in accessing practice for both support of growth and evaluation. The addition of 'growth over time' criterion was also added to explicitly allow the inclusion of examples of practice at the outset of the course to be contrasted with those from late in the year. The reflection on the two sets of teaching episodes provides the students with a better opportunity to understand their teaching and to gain a better sense of their stage of professional development. This is how the opportunities for reflection have become embedded in the structure and processes of the credential portfolio. Such conceptualisation of the portfolio process and assessment design are important considerations for the implementation of intended learning.

Practical problems

The use of portfolios for large-scale external assessment purposes is not widespread in the United States at this stage of their development (Koretz, 1998). The programmes that have been implemented have been motivated by the aims of improving teaching and learning and measuring performance. The tension associated with the different functions of assessment emerges again.

Practical difficulties identified in portfolio implementation relate to the procedures and processes of portfolio assessment. The training of teachers, raters or assessors to grade the portfolios consistently is problematic. Koretz (1998) indicates that it is more complex than other extended response forms of assessments such as essays because these tasks are uniform, presented under standard conditions and graded using consistent procedures. Tasks to be graded in portfolio assessments are not standardised. The work is accumulated during the course of teaching and learning and the conditions under which that work is produced vary. Teachers and students work with general guidelines for the selection of work to be included in the portfolio for assessment.

The American Educational Research Association has recently released a position statement concerning high-stakes testing in pre-K-12 education (AERA,

2000) because of the need to attend to conditions essential to sound implementation. In their position statement, the following conditions are considered essential to the development of an educationally sound system of student assessment particularly where this relates to high-stakes testing:

- protection against high-stakes decisions based on a single test;
- adequate resources and opportunity to learn;
- validation for each separate intended use;
- full disclosure of likely negative consequences of high-stakes testing programmes;
- alignment between the test and the curriculum;
- validity of passing scores and achievement levels;
- opportunities for meaningful remediation for examinees who fail high-stakes tests;
- appropriate attention to language differences among examinees;
- appropriate attention to students with disabilities;
- careful adherence to explicit rules for determining which students are to be tested;
- sufficient reliability for each intended use;
- ongoing evaluation of intended and unintended effects of high-stakes testing (AERA, 2000).

I would argue that these conditions apply to the use of portfolio assessment for high-stakes purposes – that is to say, when the consequences of the assessments are serious for students or for educators. This is because if the assessment system is implemented 'where educational resources are inadequate or where the assessments lack reliability and validity for their intended purposes, there is the potential for serious harm' (AERA, 2000: 2). In relation to the condition for adequate resources and opportunity to learn, it is made clear that where content standards and associated assessments are introduced to improve current practice, opportunities to access appropriate materials and development of competence with the intended changes need to occur before schools, teachers or students are sanctioned for failing to meet the new standards.

Particular attention is drawn to the need for students to have adequate opportunity to learn the content and cognitive processes to be assessed. Access to appropriate materials and development of competence with the intended changes appear to have been neglected in many attempts at the implementation of portfolios for assessment and learning purposes. It is not only teachers who need professional development to learn about the pedagogical implications for the use of portfolios for assessment and learning; students also need specific teaching and support to develop the cognitive processes of critical reflection and self-evaluation which will help them to develop a portfolio of work. Adequate time and assistance is required from their teachers. This applies to students at primary, secondary and higher levels of education, and to pre-service teachers and practitioners who find that they are required to develop a portfolio of evidence.

As has been emphasised in this book there are different types of portfolio which are dependent on the particular purpose and audience for which the portfolio is constructed. Each type, however, involves similar pedagogic practice and cognitive development. These cognitive processes include critical self-evaluation, dialogue about substantive learning issues, and reflection about learning or practice. The implications for 'portfolio pedagogy' are dialogic and interactive learning, scaffolding, collaboration, reflection and meaningful learning tasks and contexts. Brown and Campione (1990) have indicated that the students will not acquire cognitive and metacognitive strategies unless these are explicitly taught. Students therefore need to be taught about the importance of critical self-evaluation, dialogic learning and reflection in the portfolio process. They also need to be taught how to use these strategies. Time and the opportunities to modify and personalise these strategies in meaningful contexts are also required.

Salinger (1998) reports that teachers in a district in the Mid-Atlantic region of the United States moved towards reforming its assessment practices by the implementation of an early literacy portfolio. Teachers thought that the standardised test failed to reflect their students' literacy accomplishments. In this case the portfolio did not drive reform in teaching practice; rather the introduction of the literacy portfolio aimed to sustain and support improvements in classroom practice. This initiative was phased in over three years. The portfolio evolved over time with change implemented in a systematic way that enabled validation of the methodology and research into its effectiveness as an alternative to the standardised test. Despite the positive response by teachers regarding the use of portfolios for assessment purposes, various problems emerged. These related to the management of the portfolio and its component parts. They indicated that 'the process of compiling multiple documents and collecting individual records of reading and story-retelling for each child at intervals throughout the school year requires considerable organisation and time' (ibid.: 199). These demands required teachers to rethink their classroom routines and the level of individual student guidance, and to move the actual furniture in their rooms. Many teachers reconceptualised their pedagogy to integrate portfolio-related tasks and activities into their routines and everyday teaching.

Technical problems

Many of the technical problems associated with the assessment of portfolios of work stem from the nature of the tasks being assessed. Assessments of extended tasks that encourage thinking and reasoning activities raise difficulties. This is because they take time and are open to different interpretations and different types of valid response. It is therefore more difficult to ensure grading procedures that assess performance using common, general criteria (Black, 1998).

Messick (1994) has described major issues associated with the validation of performance assessments and has advocated that 'performance assessments, like all assessments should be validated in terms of content, substantive, structural, external, generalizability, and consequential aspects of construct validity' (ibid.:

22). Where possible Messick suggests that a construct-driven approach to performance assessment is used because the meaning of the construct drives the selection of relevant evidence for assessment criteria and standards. He also indicates that focusing on constructs raises the importance of construct underrepresentation and construct-irrelevant variance that are the main threats to validity.

As was discussed in the previous chapter, Heller *et al.* (1998) found examples of 'construct underrepresentation' when assessors omitted the use of important given criteria. This failure to use all intended criteria in the assessment of the portfolio of work meant that the final assessment was not based on a consideration of all the important dimensions of the construct. In their study, examples of 'construct-irrelevant variance' or instances when assessment was too broad occurred when assessors used irrelevant or idiosyncratic criteria that were not intended or included in the assessment guidelines.

Validity of inferences

A major problem identified by Koretz (1998) is establishing the validity of inferences, i.e. finding evidence that the results support the inferences that users wish to draw from them. The reasons for the invalid inferences according to Koretz are attributable to the varying degree of difficulty of tasks across portfolios. For example, a student who gains a given score on an easy task may be less proficient than a student who obtains the identical score on a more difficult task. Another reason relates to the varying amounts of assistance that students receive. Teachers vary in the amount of assistance they provide to students and this variation is carried into their management of the portfolios. Koretz indicates that in the Vermont and Kentucky portfolio programmes, teachers' practices varied in terms of the number of revisions of entries they permitted, the amount of assistance they themselves provided and the restrictions they placed on assistance from peers or other adults.

Another issue that emerges is whether the evidence in the portfolio is the student's or the pre-service teacher's own work. This can be addressed as in the case of the Scottish education system where students are required to submit a declaration that accompanies the submission to indicate that the work is their own and their teacher must also sign a statement to this effect. In the case of portfolios of work from teachers or pre-service teachers it is possible to follow up with an interview or, if a demonstration of the portfolio is required, then discussions related to the work can occur. At this stage it would be possible to ask questions to probe further about the portfolio entries. In addition, where the portfolio is embedded in a more comprehensive system of assessment, comparisons can be made with performance achievement as demonstrated during classroom observation, teacher-assessed work, tests or other assessed activities.

Generalisability

Herman *et al.* (1993) in their study of the validity of writing portfolios identified issues relevant to the large-scale use of portfolio assessment. The study raises questions about the meaningfulness and generalisability of the results obtained from portfolios and highlights some of the technical problems that need to be addressed. The researchers discovered substantial differences in students' performances when assessors made their judgements based on a standard writing assessment task, on individual samples of student work or on a portfolio collection of work. Assessors scored students' competence higher when based on the portfolio of work. They also found that assessing holistically resulted in higher scores than those based on aggregates of individually assessed samples of work. Herman *et al.* (1993) concluded that the assessments of portfolios differ depending on:

- what rating and aggregation procedures are used;
- whether the assessment is a classroom assignment or a standardised writing prompt; and
- whether analytic or holistic assessments are used to judge students' competence.

The decision to use an analytic or holistic assessment approach is dependent on the purpose of the portfolio. The Kentucky State Education Department (http://www.kde.state.ky.us/oapd/curric/publications/performanceevent/p2628.html) offers this advice. Analytic assessment guides are useful for formative purposes when incorporated in the teaching and learning cycle. The teacher in the classroom situation focuses his or her attention on obtaining as much information as possible about what students have learned and giving feedback to help students develop their understanding further. Academic expectations and content standards drive the analytic assessment. The advantages of such an approach include feedback to students about their performance; effective analysis of individual student progress and needs; guidance on very specific content and processes; and the organisation of a matrix if multiple elements are being assessed.

The holistic assessment approach is suitable when teachers need to assign an overall grade or score to a series of performance tasks or multiple portfolio entries. Holistic assessment guides are used when a final evaluation is required. They are usually more efficient and provide a final grade for the complete portfolio. This approach is most effective when all the entries in the portfolio are closely related. Teachers need to be careful that when they use a holistic assessment guide they are clear about what it is they intend to assess.

Reliability

Koretz (1998) defines reliability as the consistency of measurement. He states that to be meaningful measurement must be reasonably consistent and replicable. He examined the quality of the performance data produced by large-scale portfolio assessments (referred to above) and concluded that the evaluations of reliability that focused on consistency of scoring produced highly variable results. To illustrate, the reliability of the marking was low, with unsatisfactory agreement between different markers and, in mathematics, large variation in the performance of a student from one task to another. He also found that scores from portfolio assessments often do not show anticipated relationships with other achievement data. Koretz concluded that the current stage of development of portfolio assessment in the United States is problematic for large-scale external assessment.

Supovitz *et al.* (1997) in their examination of inter-rater reliability of arts portfolio assessment in the primary grades identified three weaknesses associated with the portfolio system that impacted on the attainment of high levels of reliability. Two of these problems were associated with the portfolio policies of the district and the other was associated with the classroom-level implementation. The first problem related to the insufficient evidence available in the reading portfolios for external assessors to determine the level of students' reading skills. By increasing the number of pieces required and their forms, that is, more than just paper-and-pencil evidence, both the quantity and quality of evidence available for external reviewers was expanded. The second problem related to the lack of clear links between the stages of development that serve as the criteria for student work and the evidence in the form of pieces of student work in the portfolios. This impacted on the accuracy of external assessors' judgements. The third problem involved the teachers who failed to provide the necessary portfolio pieces for external assessors to make judgements. This particular study highlights the different nature of the technical problems that can occur and that require careful consideration in the design, phases of development and implementation of a portfolio assessment system.

Resourcing

Another major problem associated with portfolio implementation is the significant resources required, ranging from the training of teachers to grade the portfolios, the support for students to comprehend the portfolio processes, the development of resources to support implementation, increased workload for teachers and excessive demands on their time. Stecher (1998) notes that these resource implications continue even when teachers become more experienced and confident.

The assessment of portfolios adds significantly to teachers' workloads. The initial training and professional development to prepare teachers for the assessment tasks takes time. The extent of work to be assessed and the administration burden contribute to teacher workload. The accompanying pedagogical changes also require careful planning, changes to lessons and more time. These related tasks of creating curriculum-embedded assessments and developing communities of assessors for inter-rater reliability purposes can be powerful professional development opportunities. The increased workload for teachers needs to be acknowledged and supported if the benefits are to be sustained.

Stone (1998) examined the impact of portfolio construction on student learning and reflection in two groups of pre-service teachers at California State University, Fresno in the US, who had differing levels of guidance in portfolio preparation and development. The principal problems identified for the students were the lack of time they had to develop the portfolio given that the programme required much coursework and pre-service teaching. They were confused and had limited understanding of the process; they also felt they did not get the assistance they needed from their supervisors and they experienced difficulty in collecting and selecting artefacts. The writing of reflections also proved problematic. The major pitfalls that hindered the portfolio construction related to the developmental nature of the portfolio process. Students gradually need to learn about portfolios and gain an understanding of portfolio construction and the habit of reflection on practice. Supervisors also need to be knowledgable and experienced in these processes.

Tensions

Broadfoot (1998a) in analysing the Records of Achievement (RoA) (portfolios) initiative in England and Wales outlines the difficulties for policy-makers in handling the tensions associated with the varying purposes of assessment. Governments must confront the major tension that exists in the well-established role of assessment for certification and selection purposes and the more recent emphasis on assessment for formative purposes. Broadfoot indicates that the RoA initiative emerged as a reaction to the shortcomings of existing assessment methods and the search for more 'authentic' modes and more useful ways of reporting evidence about student achievement. Developments in assessment have been linked to learning. For example, self-assessment, action-planning, target-setting, recording and portfolio preparation are all intended to enhance learning. Broadfoot (1998b: 5) concludes 'the persistence of approaches to assessment which were conceived and implemented in response to the social and educational needs of a very different era, effectively prevents any real progress'.

Wolf (1998) has analysed the portfolio assessment of National Vocational Qualifications and General National Vocational Qualifications in England and Wales. In this analysis she illustrates clearly why the system failed to deliver on its promises. The reasons she identifies were not attributable to the concept of portfolios, as such, but more to do with the way in which the assessment of the portfolio was conceived and the assessment scheme adopted. She emphasises that the attempt to describe the intended learning outcomes so that they were transparent or clear to assessors, assessees and third parties resulted in problems of manageability and the reliability of assessor judgements. The National Council for Vocational Qualifications required that evidence be provided in the portfolio for all performance criteria and all components of the range, i.e. the areas of skills, knowledge and understanding of a particular unit of a subject. The clarity and detail with which the outcomes were specified took on a 'tightly regulated form'. The belief that tight national standards could be communicated by detailed outcome specification and that it was desirable and feasible to require exhaustive evidence rather than sampling was the problem. As Wolf explains, detailed written standards do not guarantee reliable or valid assessment practice. What has been established is that tacit knowledge, professional judgement and assessors' development of understanding of the standards are more useful (Wolf, 1993). The problems that emerged were related to the heavy requirement for evidence in the GNVQ portfolios. Students became 'hunters and gatherers' of information and many saw their major responsibility as locating and collecting information. Many also saw the attainment of the qualification as their major objective and developed 'coping strategies'. To illustrate, some students wrote action plans after the work was completed, others resorted to 'creative copying', and as they became familiar with the criteria they learned to use them mechanistically. Such behaviour worked against the intended form of learning. The assessment system was perceived as complex, difficult to organise and manage with heavy paperwork for the planning, implementation and assessment of work. As a result students felt themselves to be under constant pressure and demotivated. An identified cause for non-completion of the course was the inability of students to maintain the steady rate of portfolio development.

What is apparent from this analysis is how the intended learning can become trivialised and mindless as a consequence of an attempt to standardise the assessment procedure and the judgements by the use of highly specified standards. The intention was to make the award transparent to employers and other 'users' so that the comprehensive accumulation of evidence in the portfolio would allow the candidate to demonstrate competence on every single component of the award. In specifying the standards and the assessment criteria it was intended that the reliability and comparability across institutions and assessors were assured. Internal and external verifiers were seen as important additional sources of quality control. However, in reality the value of verification for either promoting assessment reliability or improving the quality of the programmes was seen as limited. The criticism levelled at the NVQ and GNVQ assessment systems, as has been discussed, has resulted in a reduction in the part played by portfolios in the overall assessment and a move to sampling of key features rather than demonstrating everything.

Accountability pressures

The major obstacle to the spread of portfolios is the accountability function of assessments, i.e. selection, certification and accountability for student performance at school or district levels. The growth of educational accountability policies and politicians' demands for precise measures constrain the widespread implementation of portfolios for assessment purposes. For it is in this context that issues of reliability and precision and their impact on the education system are emphasised. There is a continuing tension between an emphasis on learning and motivation and the demands for cost-effective and established mechanisms for selection, allocation and accountability. In the broadening of the evidential base for assessment the relativities of purpose, time, preparation and resources govern the extent to which portfolio use for learning and assessment purposes is realised.

Assessment, as is evident in this chapter, communicates important messages to students about what learning outcomes are valued, what the major curriculum priorities are, how they should manage their time and how they should see themselves as learners (Broadfoot, 1996). The introduction of a portfolio system of assessment offers an alternative to current practice that has the potential to foster important learning. However, in the design and implementation of the portfolio system there is also potential for problems, as has been illustrated by past experiences. This chapter has concentrated on analysing these problems and tensions involved in implementing portfolio assessment systems. With the emphasis on the initial problems experienced in different contexts the reader could well be thinking, 'If portfolios cause so many problems, what is the point of the whole enterprise?' Very few long-term studies about the impact of portfolios exist. Much of what has been written has focused on the issues associated with establishing a portfolio system. To capitalise on the benefits of portfolios there is a need to learn from these early experiences and to create a view of assessment that positions the portfolio as central. This requires policy-match to purpose and paradigm. The conceptual issues are also significant and these range from teaching the importance of assessment for learning to shifting current thinking about assessment, and to the actual conceptualisation of the portfolio in the context in which it will be implemented.

The next chapter takes the form of a case study which tells how a portfolio system was implemented in one department of a teacher education institution. It will recount how some of the problems highlighted in this chapter emerged and what efforts were put in place to deal with them.

Summary

- Most attempts to design, develop and implement a portfolio assessment system have encountered problems that have resulted from unhelpful policy decisions, conceptual confusions, practical or technical problems.
- Major problems associated with new assessment forms such as the portfolio arise from a mismatch of purpose to paradigm, curriculum design or pedagogic practices.
- The prevailing understanding of the nature and purpose of assessment can militate against the success of portfolio use by distorting the associated teaching and learning processes.
- Teachers need to engage in professional development that will support the integration of new assessment systems into the curriculum and their teaching practice, and the policy context needs to be supportive of such change.
- Students need specific teaching and support to develop the cognitive processes of critical reflection and self-evaluation that help them to develop a portfolio of work.
- Technical problems encountered in the assessment of the portfolio include: validity of inferences, generalisability, reliability and resourcing.
- In the assessment of the portfolio construct, underrepresentation and construct irrelevant variance are the main threats to validity.

5   A case study

This chapter is based on a case study of an attempt to use portfolios for assessment and learning purposes in an initial-teacher education course. A pilot programme was carried out initially, the research continued and progressive refocusing led to an investigation of the extent to which the use of portfolios promoted the development of important teaching and learning skills such as reflective practice.

The reason for including this case study is to share with readers the developmental process in the implementation of a portfolio and the implications for pedagogy and learning. It is also an opportunity to reflect on these processes and provide insights on the procedures, practices and resources involved. The lessons learnt from the experience are described and the implications expanded for others to consider in their own attempts to set up and implement portfolio systems for assessment.

It is important to teach assessment in teacher education courses as it relates to teaching and learning. Pre-service teachers need to know how to develop assessment and pedagogic practices that require students to be actively engaged in their learning and to encourage them to take responsibility for that learning. The more general implication for teacher educators is that they need to ensure that pre-service teachers have the opportunities to develop the reflective capacity that will enable them to keep pace with important developments in assessment. They need to know the vital links between assessment and the teaching and learning cycle. A way to understand the value of an educational model of assessment and to develop the ability to implement assessment strategies to align with this model is to engage with such practice at pre-service level. If pre-service teachers are to learn how to use these methods with children then they need to have some experience of them. Pre-service teachers need to be *participant observers* of these new forms of assessment. They need to reflect and self-evaluate as part of the assessment practice for their own learning but also to understand the importance of an educational model of assessment. This context provided the impetus for using portfolios for assessment of pre-service teachers' learning in two modules completed in their first year of teacher training.

Portfolio processes and intended learning

The pre-service teachers involved in this case study were in their first year of a two-year course. The development of a portfolio of work was a requirement of their study of two modules: 'Classroom Teaching Skills', a very practically orientated module, and 'Instructional Design and Strategies for Effective Teaching' which was more theoretical. Both modules were assessed summatively by means of a portfolio of work. However, during the course the portfolio was being constructed and assessed formatively for purposes of supporting important learning that was taking place in the schools during teaching practice and at the educational institution where they were studying.

The module 'Classroom Teaching Skills' aimed to provide pre-service teachers with principles and strategies that would enable them to make appropriate practical decisions in the teaching and learning activities of the classroom. Specifically, on completion of the module they were expected to:

- apply communication principles;
- demonstrate presentation skills;
- describe the structure and components of lesson plans;
- develop detailed lesson plans and schemes of work;
- evaluate lesson plans;
- describe various teaching strategies (expository, discussion, inquiry, discovery etc.) and evaluate their importance;
- suggest reasons for misbehaviour;
- demonstrate skills in classroom management.

For the module 'Instructional Design and Strategies for Effective Teaching' students were expected to:

- provide a statement of personal philosophy, goals and core values;
- provide an evaluation of their own teaching in order to improve it;
- establish expectations for students that are clear, challenging and achievable;
- teach students according to their diverse talents and interests;
- plan teaching on the basis of recent learning theory;
- align teaching objectives, content, teaching method and assessment;
- make effective use of different means of grouping students;
- motivate and engage students in learning;
- develop sound routine procedures to manage recurring tasks; and
- respond appropriately to situations that may arise incidentally.

These pre-service teachers were informed that they would need to collect samples of work that they felt reflected their attainment of these particular skills and competencies. Suggestions about the type of evidence for the intended learning outcomes for the modules were identified and discussed. To illustrate, for the learning outcome 'Provide a statement of personal philosophy, goals and core values' it was suggested that the type of evidence that might be selected for inclusion in the portfolio could be:

- a concept map that outlines your central beliefs as a teacher;
- a video clip that demonstrates your values as depicted in the teaching and learning strategies you choose to use;
- a paper that clearly describes your central beliefs as a teacher;
- a photographic display of teaching or learning practices, which has been annotated to reflect your goals as a teacher.

In addition to providing a piece of evidence of the above type, pre-service teachers were also expected to provide an accompanying reflective statement. They were instructed that the reflective statement should analyse and illustrate how they thought that the evidence they had selected demonstrated their competence. In an excerpt from one such reflective statement a pre-service teacher wrote:

> As a teacher I value and emphasise critical thinking. This kind of reflective education not only teaches students basic subject knowledge but also teaches them how to make intelligent choices in all areas of their lives.
>
> I believe deeply that every student has some good qualities regardless of his or her academic achievement. Therefore to become a responsible and helpful teacher I should match my teaching strategies with my students' learning styles, so as to motivate their learning, and develop their talents and potential to the fullest (this may not be academic). [Refer to the video clip of my teaching practice where I used teaching strategies to match my students' learning styles.]
>
> Another personal belief of mine is that I do not always consider the best academic performer as the best student, rather I prefer to assess my students individually by examining the progress they are making in academic achievement as well as in other areas of performance. For example, I value the student who is less able to perform academically yet who strives hard to achieve, compared with the student who is gifted and does not put in the effort and gets a slightly better grade. I believe that a student's willingness to learn and the effort he or she puts into the work counts (process) more than the grade (outcome). If the process were not valued then education would be meaningless in the sense that students are just mechanically performing what they are capable of doing without attending to the actual process of learning.
>
> (Pre-service teacher portfolio, 1997)

It was in this way pre-service teachers developed portfolios of work to demonstrate their achievements. The procedures and processes adopted to achieve the use of portfolios for assessment and learning purposes will now be described more fully.

Procedures adopted for portfolio use

At this formative stage of portfolio use in this teacher education institute there was only one department involved in their use for assessment and learning. Only two modules studied by the pre-service teachers who were in their first year of a two-year course were involved. The pre-service teachers were expected to draw on their teaching practice to demonstrate their competence in teaching skills and reflective practice, relevant to the aims of the two modules taught by this department.

At the commencement of the module lecturers explained the importance of the learning objectives and emphasised that the assessment system to be used was criterion-referenced. They gave pre-service teachers the set of grade descriptors used for assessing portfolio work (see Figure 5.1). Lecturers' expectations, such as the need for pre-service teachers to present their findings, to attend an interview with their lecturer, to understand the criteria for assessment and to be aware of the grade descriptors, were made explicit at the outset.

To assist the pre-service teachers in developing an understanding of the concept of the teaching portfolio the following specific strategies were used:

- A video that outlined the meaning, the requirements and the assessment of portfolios was shown.
- Teaching portfolios developed by pre-service teachers in the previous year were shared and exemplars were highlighted to indicate the standards required.
- Detailed explanations of what should be included and what should not be included were given.
- Pre-service teachers were then encouraged to explain what the teaching portfolio meant to them.

At the outset the pre-service teachers had difficulty conceptualising what a portfolio was. A typical comment was: 'At the beginning, I had no idea what it was all about. I thought it was as simple as filing my data. However, this doesn't seem to be the case. I realised that the portfolio was more than just a filing system' (pre-service teacher interview, 1997). Over time the procedures and the lecturers' explanations appeared to have some impact on some pre-service teachers' understanding of the requirements. 'There were some explanations from the teacher that we need to be doing some reflection and presentation. We were shown a video of how to prepare a portfolio, we were also told that we should be continuously collecting information for our own portfolio' (pre-service teacher interview, 1997).

From interview data it was evident that the lecturers had identified the following necessary skills that pre-service teachers needed to develop their portfolios effectively:

- independent study skills;
- ability to work as a group member;
- self-assessment strategies;
- self-monitoring skills;
- ability to self-evaluate; and
- questioning skills.

Figure 5.1 Grade descriptors used to grade the portfolio of work

GRADE DESCRIPTORS

Grade A Distinction
- The evidence for the portfolio is of outstanding and exceptional quality in all respects and surpasses the objectives of the module.
- The reflective statements demonstrate deep and original thinking, interpretation, critical thinking and synthesis. Cogent arguments are used and supported by well-selected references.
- The work is well structured, is expressed with flair and there is little or no redundancy.
- The grade is an expression of confidence in the ability of the student to progress as an independent learner.

Grade B Credit
- The evidence selected for the portfolio surpasses the objectives for the module and demonstrates a sound understanding of content.
- Arguments are used in the reflective statements to support the student's point of view and references are used appropriately.
- The work is well structured, well organised, written fluently and correctly documented.
- The grade is an expression of confidence in the ability of the student to progress with some supervision and guidance.

Grade C Pass
- The evidence selected for the portfolio achieves the objectives for the module, and demonstrates an adequate grasp of the content, but is confined to the minimum requirement.
- There is little evidence of independent reflection in the reflective statements and research is superficial with a minimum attempt at analysis and/or synthesis.
- The work is lacking in organisation and the language is reasonably fluent but has some lapses in grammar and syntax.
- The grade is an expression of confidence in the ability of the student to go further with normal supervision and guidance.

Grade D Fail
- The evidence selected for the portfolio does not adequately meet the objectives for the module.
- The reflective statement is a simple recall of facts with little or no evidence of research or documentation. There is no effort to supplement evidence with own critical reflections.
- The work is poorly structured, poorly organised and lacks consistency.
- The grade is an expression that the student may resubmit but will find higher level work very difficult. (Students granted a supplementary assessment can qualify for no more than a Pass Grade of C.)

Grade E Clear Fail
- The evidence selected does not achieve the objectives for the module and demonstrates little understanding of the content of the module.
- The reflective statements make assertions without supportive evidence and arguments.
- The work does not meet the minimum levels of presentation for this module: there are major and frequent mistakes in written expression. The work does not address the stated requirements and is not organised in an obvious manner.

Source: Portfolio Use in Initial Teacher Education: A Student Guide. Hong Kong, Hong Kong Institute of Education, 1997.

After reviewing the pre-service teachers' first efforts, all the lecturers involved agreed that they showed little initiative or inclination to take responsibility for their own learning. For example, 'They [pre-service teachers] found it very difficult to accept the idea that they might have to put in things of their own, other than what I would tell them to do . . . I told them that they must have findings of their own' (Lecturer interview, 1997).

The need for pedagogic changes when using a portfolio for assessment and learning purposes became obvious. This was particularly the case in this context where a psychometric paradigm had dominated assessment practices. Lecturers indicated that their teaching incorporated the following changes:

- dialogic learning where the lecturer shared ideas and promoted discussion rather than lecturing and giving notes;
- tutorials, interviews and one-to-one sessions with the pre-service teachers;
- discussion groups and peer critique; and
- more diversity of teaching styles with emphasis on cognitive growth and inquiry training.

More specific and significant impacts on lecturer teaching styles were identified from an analysis of the interview data, the video-recordings and observations of lessons. There was far greater facilitation of learning and less exam orientation; more efficient time management with discussion groups and peer critique; increased flexibility and freedom to adapt and change teaching styles; changes in pedagogic approaches and style; guidance to pre-service teachers in the developmental process; responsibility to pre-service teachers for the collection and selection of work for the portfolio; and trust in pre-service teachers to work collaboratively.

One lecturer commented that the major impact on his teaching had been:

> constantly thinking of what you have to do . . . what order of things you can do them in and how you can get the students to change their way of going through a lesson, or presenting a lesson. I am constantly aware of what I should be doing in all these things to impact on portfolio use. There was a lot of impact on my teaching.
>
> (Lecturer interview, 1997)

Lecturers noted that they were more interested in their own teaching and were keen to use portfolios after the previous year's pilot experience. Several lecturers suggested that the pedagogic practice required for the implementation of portfolios reflected their own philosophy of teaching, which was characterised by a belief in active student engagement in the learning process. Lecturers who had implemented portfolios the previous year stated they had a better understanding of the grading process and the standards. Consequently they were able to give pre-service teachers more detailed, and clearer explanations and feedback on ways to improve the presentation of their work.

Impact on the development of skills

Lecturers explained that the portfolio developed for the module 'Classroom Teaching Skills' required pre-service teachers to focus on the practical skills of lesson-planning, presenting, questioning, managing student behaviour and teaching strategies. Pre-service teachers were required to comment on their under-standing and development of these skills in their portfolios, to use these skills and demonstrate their learning during teaching practice and then reflect on these experiences in their portfolios.

As an illustration, this excerpt is taken from a pre-service teacher's portfolio. It is one aspect of a reflective statement included in the portfolio to demonstrate the development of self-evaluation skills. The reflective statement was completed after the pre-service teacher had studied the module 'Classroom Teaching Skills' and completed a teaching practice of six weeks.

> Although the lesson plan for the group charcoal drawing of the lesson of F2E[1] was not much of a problem the lesson failed to meet the objectives since one of the most essential, yet elusive, elements in teaching is missing – the students' interest.
>
> I believe that it is important for me, as a teacher, to understand the preference/interest, as well as the ability of the students, before/while planning a lesson; and whenever necessary, change/adjust the objectives/planning/ways of instruction to match the learning styles of a particular group of students in order to motivate them to participate in class.
>
> (Pre-service teacher portfolio, 1997)

All lecturers noted that for some of the pre-service teachers there was more self-learning evident through this experience. One lecturer commented how

> after teaching practice [pre-service teachers] were able to reflect on their teaching practice and apply their new learning to the classroom teaching skills. They showed the relationship of this training [sic] with the skills they have learned from the classroom . . . I think it was a good indication that some of the [pre-service teachers] realised that they can use their freedom to do what they want with their portfolio.
>
> (Lecturer interview, 1997)

From analyses of the portfolios it was clear that pre-service teachers were reflecting and integrating their understanding of the learning and teaching theories discussed in their lessons. For example, one student commented on how the importance of different learning styles was realised.

> The concept of learning style reminds me that my students are different – this helps me to become more sensitive to individual differences in behaviour and learning. I am less apt to interpret the differences as unimportant or

inappropriate. The classroom can become a model of tolerance and the learning climate improves (thus enhancing students' learning).

Different learning styles suggest the need to vary my instruction – alternations such as individual projects, small group discussions, cooperative learning, and learning centres provide a flexibility in meeting individual student's learning needs (Pre-service teacher interview, 1997).

Analyses of the lecturers' observations, recordings and portfolios supported the interview data obtained from the pre-service teachers. The use of portfolios helps pre-service teachers take responsibility for their learning. 'Portfolio encouraged me to take greater responsibility for my own learning because I learned how to assess what I have learned best' (Pre-service teacher interview, 1997).

According to the lecturers interviewed and the analyses of the video-recordings of the pre-service teachers' performance assessments, the use of portfolios for assessment purposes appeared to have a positive impact on pre-service teachers' approaches to learning in the following ways:

- in-depth study;
- detailed presentations;
- active learning;
- independent learning;
- developmental and individually paced learning;
- awareness of own learning;
- motivation to participate;
- improved attendance;
- interest in their own achievements and performance;
- consultation with lecturers regarding their own learning; and
- interest in grading and assessment process.

The pre-service teachers who were interviewed indicated that the use of portfolios had helped them develop reflective thinking. 'I can see substantial change in the ways I think about my own thinking. I had begun to look at the course from a different viewpoint' (Pre-service teacher interview, 1997). Another pre-service teacher commented: 'I learned more from the portfolio than from the lessons. Completing this assignment was harsh work, but it really helped me organise my learning and thinking' (Pre-service teacher interview, 1997).

The following learning outcomes emerged from pre-service teachers' experience of developing and presenting a portfolio of work. They were identified from an analysis of all data collected for the case study:

- organisational skills;
- evaluation and self-evaluation skills;
- increased reflective capacity;
- integration of procedural and declarative knowledge;
- understanding of preferred learning styles;

- independent learning and more self-reliance;
- improved learning,
- more accurate and comprehensive memory of readings and researched topics;
- group participation skills and greater cooperation;
- action planning; and
- impact on self-concept and enhanced personal growth.

Constraints and problems

Lecturers and pre-service teachers identified numerous difficulties and constraints associated with the use of portfolios for assessment purposes in this setting. Many of these problems related to the assessment procedures themselves as well as the grading system. There was a need to develop greater inter-rater reliability by meeting more regularly to develop a community of understanding of the standards looked for and to adopt a more consistent approach to the grading of the portfolios.

A clearer framework and specific guidelines were requested. It was indicated that this would help pre-service teachers understand what was required of them. Lecturers wanted a better understanding of what constituted an A grade portfolio, more exemplars, more specific criteria and more examples to illustrate the standards. To address these needs a set of guidelines and an interactive CD ROM were developed to be used as an implementation resource for future courses.

Guidelines

The guidelines developed provided suggestions for the introduction and implementation of portfolio use for assessment and learning. These guidelines were intended for all staff and for the pre-service teachers who elsewhere might also want to use portfolios in their teaching and assessment practices.

It was suggested that, because portfolios might be a new concept, it was important to provide a thorough explanation and clear guidelines. The following suggestions to raise awareness about portfolios were given.

- Use teaching aids such as videos to outline the background, the theory, the processes and procedures involved in the use of portfolios. Provide the students with sample portfolios to help them understand the format, evidence and standards required.
- Provide students with guidelines that make the expectations of portfolio use explicit. Outline the design of the portfolio, the competencies or learning outcomes the student is required to demonstrate and the indicators of attainment that the student may choose to include in the portfolio.
- Share the assessment process with the students by discussing the criteria to be used. Clarify the grade descriptors and share exemplars with students to help them understand the standard required. Provide students with feedback for formative purposes during stages of development of the portfolio. Use progress

maps or learning continua to indicate clearly where students are demonstrating competence and where they need to develop and improve.

- Explain the developmental nature of the portfolio and the need to collect baseline data. For example, facilitate student video-recording of important stages of their development. Allow students time to reflect, self-evaluate, practise their portfolio presentations.

- Encourage students to present their portfolios and demonstrate their learning. Discuss and critique student performance. Students will come to understand the standards through presentation and small- or large-scale group discussion. Allow students to work collaboratively and encourage peer critique and evaluation. Ensure groups discuss early in the course and throughout as needed.

In the guidelines developed it was stated that the portfolio documents the students' achievements over an extended period and reflects careful, critical self-evaluation. For each competency the student was informed that supporting evidence plus a reflective statement would be required to enable assessment to occur. The student was advised to select evidence to demonstrate achievement of competence from a range of materials chosen from their learning and teaching contexts. Suggestions included: research papers, assignments, lesson plans, schemes of work, video clips, photographs, samples of students' work and self-evaluations.

The structure of the portfolio described in the guidelines emphasised the need for a self-evaluation that would enable the student to analyse her own learning during the course and identify implications for her own action. For the lecturer important information concerning the student's teaching and learning experiences would be apparent from this type of self-evaluation.

The evidence and connecting reflective statements were emphasised and outlined in detail. It was stressed that students would need to be taught how to develop reflective practice and how to select valid, reliable and adequate evidence in support of claims. The guidelines suggested that the lecturer would explain clearly and carefully the expectations and the criteria to be used in assessing the portfolio. The reflective statement was limited to one A4 page and there was one required per competency. To help students understand the way in which they might go about developing their reflective statements, an example was given in relation to the competency 'Provide a statement of personal philosophy, goals and core values'. It was suggested that to demonstrate that the student had attained this competency the reflective statement could include a discussion of the student's central values as a teacher. These values would develop from students' reading about teaching and learning styles, from their own experiences of teaching/learning and/or from their cultural backgrounds. It was suggested that they discuss the views they have formed about teaching and learning styles and theories, teacher–student relationships and values they believe underpin their personal beliefs as a teacher. Suggestions of evidence to support claims were given.

For the purpose of assessment it was suggested that construction of the portfolio would begin from the outset of the semester and continue for the duration. At the early stages of development it was suggested that students receive formative feedback from the lecturer about their learning and possible ways to improve. The criteria to be used in the assessment of the portfolio should be shared with the students at the outset of the course. To help students understand the grade-related criteria and the standards required it was suggested that the lecturers share exemplars of students' work for illustrative purposes. Formative feedback from the outset would also help the student determine the acceptable quality of work expected. The grade descriptors presented in Figure 5.1 were used.

Supports

The supports that were provided to lecturers can be summarised as follows. A set of guidelines were developed and included:

- suggestions for introduction and implementation of the portfolio process;
- a framework for the portfolio;
- learning outcomes and suggestions of evidence suitable to address these outcomes;
- advice regarding self-evaluations and reflective statements;
- criteria to be used in the assessment of the portfolios;
- grade descriptors; and
- exemplars that illustrate standards.

An interactive CD ROM was also developed for implementation purposes. Included on the CD ROM were the identified principles for portfolio use and exemplar material from pre-service teacher portfolios.

Time is needed to meet with colleagues to clarify understanding and to exchange ideas about implementing the portfolio processes and procedures. Lecturers also need professional development to develop their pedagogic and assessment practices. Colleagues need to be familiar with the criteria and to share portfolio exemplars to develop an understanding of the standards required.

The pre-service teachers need to be familiar with the concept of the portfolio and be clear about expectations. They need to know what the assessment process entails and how assessment will occur both formatively and summatively. They need to be familiar with the assessment criteria.

Role of the lecturers: portfolio pedagogy

This level of support will require some change to the pedagogic practice of the lecturer. If reflective statements and self-evaluation are an important aspect of the portfolio then pre-service teachers will need to be taught how to engage in these practices. As has been outlined in previous chapters substantive dialogue, scaffolding, collaboration, interactive and dialogic and meaningful learning activities and environments are important elements of effective teaching to achieve these purposes. Brown and Campione's (1990) research indicates that less capable students do not acquire a variety of cognitive and metacognitive strategies unless they are taught and given detailed and explicit instruction on how to acquire these learning strategies. The more complex the strategy to be learned, the more explicit the instruction needs to be for all students. The portfolio process described in this book requires reflection and self-evaluation so here is an opportunity for pre-service teachers to be taught strategies that they can make their own through modifying and personalising them within a meaningful context and learning environment. This is a reflective, flexible use of a strategy that is helping the individual construct learning forward.

In using portfolios with the pre-service teachers, lecturers made pedagogic changes to facilitate the development of the intended learning outcomes. The portfolio pedagogy that emerged could be characterised by the following changes:

- a practical approach to development and application of skills relevant to subject content (i.e. lesson planning, presentation, questioning and evaluation);
- team and group work;
- active listening;
- consistent feedback;
- video-recordings of pre-service teachers' presentations of their learning;
- video-recordings of pre-service teachers' teaching practice experience; and
- reflections and evaluations of learning and practical experiences.

Such changes helped provide a learning environment for pre-service teachers which was characterised by:

- a focus on progress and improvement;
- participation;
- interaction and exchange of ideas;
- deeper understanding;
- enjoyment and satisfaction (for both pre-service teachers and their lecturers);
- initiative;
- communication; and
- comfort.

According to some lecturers this environment encouraged pre-service teachers to accept advice and criticism from their peers and lecturers. The provision of this and other feedback on a regular and consistent basis impacted on learning. 'I have given them a lot of feedback on their immature way of performance and I have some small-group talks during my class. I think the students have benefited because they valued the idea of learning from each other' (Lecturer interview, 1997). Lecturers indicated that the impact on learning was to increase pre-service teachers' confidence, 'sophistication in their thinking' and 'interaction with their answers'.

Some pre-service teachers' perceptions about their learning resonate with those of the lecturers. 'I was doing some reflection as I go along. There was independent sorting of information at the end of the day. I included notes from my reading and evaluated the different skills' (Pre-service teacher interview, 1997). Another pre-service teacher added how she now reflected more frequently to help integrate learning: 'I normally reflect (on my work) every few weeks – topic by topic. Then I make an overall reflection at the end of the module. It was more of a progressive learning to me' (Pre-service teacher interview, 1997).

Important learning occurred not only for the pre-service teachers but also for the team of lecturers involved in this two-year project. Many of the problems and pitfalls outlined in the previous chapter emerged as the concept of a portfolio was developing at the same time as it was being piloted and researched. For the majority of the team, learning about assessment and integrating it with teaching and learning required more support than was available. The development of implementation resources proved valuable in the second year as pedagogic practices evolved so that they were more aligned with the use of portfolios for learning and assessment. The team's involvement in the pilot study contributed significantly to the development of a community of shared practices. It was important to meet to discuss the assessment procedures and to share portfolios of work to understand the standards and to develop more consistent grading approaches.

Making the move from an assessment practice based on examinations and short-answer tests to the use of portfolios required professional development. Important principles emerged from the study and these were helpful in illustrating the ways in which changes to curriculum design, assessment and pedagogic practices needed to occur. These principles are discussed fully in the next chapter.

Summary

- Findings from this case study concluded that to develop portfolios students need skills in independent study, group work, self-monitoring, self-assessment, self-evaluation and questioning.
- Pedagogic changes required when introducing the use of portfolios include: dialogic learning, tutorials, interviews, one-to-one sessions, discussion groups, peer critique, diversity of teaching styles, emphasis on cognitive growth and inquiry training.
- The impact of the use of portfolios on learning included an increase in: in-depth study, detailed presentations, active learning, independent learning, developmental and individually paced learning, awareness of own learning strategies, motivation to participate, improved attendance, interest in own achievements and performance, consultation with lecturers regarding own learning, interest in grading and assessment practices.
- Problems experienced related to the assessment procedures and the grading system. There was a need for greater inter-rater reliability through regular meetings to develop a community of understanding of the standards required and to adopt a more consistent approach to the grading of the portfolios.
- Supports for the implementation of a portfolio system include: guidelines for the introduction and implementation of the portfolio process, a framework

for the portfolio, intended learning outcomes and suggestions for suitable evidence, advice regarding self-evaluations and reflective statements, criteria to be used in the assessment of the portfolios, grade descriptors and exemplars that illustrate the standards.

6 Possibilities and principles

This chapter begins by describing the possibilities of using the portfolio for professional preparation, appraisal and promotion purposes. The role of the portfolio for improvement of one's effectiveness in one's profession or to demonstrate professional knowledge for career advancement is elaborated by reference to examples from the medical and teaching professions. The principles that underpin the use of portfolios for learning and assessment purposes conclude the chapter. The six principles emerged from the research described in chapter 5 and each is discussed in relation to research findings and a review of the literature. Important implications for educators and policy-makers are offered as an attempt to disseminate and extend the debate for more alternative forms of assessment such as the portfolio.

Possibilities

Portfolios are being used increasingly for professional preparation and appraisal purposes. For promotional purposes teachers, lecturers and administrators are being asked to present a portfolio of evidence. The role of the portfolio in career advancement, to demonstrate professional knowledge and as a strategy to improve one's effectiveness as a professional, lecturer, teacher or administrator is discussed and illustrated.

Portfolios for professional development

Portfolios and their contribution to the professional development of General Practitioners (GPs) will be examined first. A portfolio used for learning enables GPs to focus on their experiences through reflections on their work. Learning and work are not seen as separate experiences; they are interwoven in the portfolio process. Everyday achievements, problems and concerns of the GP are integrated into the learning as reflected upon in the portfolio. It is also possible for the GP to tailor the learning programme to her or his learning style and needs rather than accepting set educational programmes. GPs can engage in learning that meets their own self-identified needs and at a stage and manner considered appropriate. Choices that meet the individual's learning style and the practical constraints under which the individual is working can be accommodated. To illustrate, a GP who identifies the need to acquire more skills in giving feedback can be addressed through a professional development programme and then those skills can be put into practice. Evidence of achievements can be produced, recorded and reflected upon for the portfolio. The portfolio can accommodate a range of learning styles and varied learning needs, requiring different learning experiences. Further examples given by Pietroni and Millard (1997:86) include:

- a need for clinical knowledge such as information about the potential and applications of a new drug;
- managerial needs such as skills of team-building and needs related to interpersonal skills; and
- attitudes such as those required for working with families of terminally ill children.

In this way the portfolio is learner-centred, focusing on the individual's identified needs. Once these needs have been identified the individual has an idea of what she hopes to gain, the chosen method for learning, evaluation and reflection on what has been learned. There is a shift from attending to the content to a reflective consideration of the value of the learning achieved.

The autonomy of the learner and her or his ability to develop her or his own professional development programme are respected. The learner together with the help of a mentor or facilitator identifies strengths and areas for development. The mentor offers support and guidance on areas for extension and challenge while the learner remains responsible for the learning. The portfolio offers a structure to manage learning needs, to capture learning experiences in the workplace and encourages self-directed learning. For trainees the portfolio can incorporate videos of demonstrations of skill acquisition at various stages, projects, diaries, journals encouraging reflective learning. Trainees assume responsibility for their own learning and build habits of reflection and analysis appropriate for continuing and self-initiated professional development. Dependency on the trainer or a more experienced other is not encouraged.

In researching the use of portfolios for learning in the context of general practice, Pietroni and Millard (1997: 90) found that mentors require the ability to:

- provide support;
- help the learner identify their strengths;
- help the learner identify their needs;
- help the learner set educational plans;
- encourage and facilitate reflection; and
- use responding skills such as active listening, reflection and feedback.

The use of portfolios in this context involves the identification by the learner of an experience that has a direct bearing on her or his professional role as a GP. The use of critical incidents or case analysis is helpful in choosing the particular experience on which to focus. The mentor encourages the individual to describe the experience fully and then to reflect on it to identify the learning that has occurred. The mentor facilitates this process by clarifying, summarising and reflecting back to the learner. Important needs for continuing professional development are identified and educational plans are set up with the help of the mentor. These plans include details of learning objectives, learning resources, strategies with an indication of how the learning will be achieved and assessed. The learner evaluates the quality of the process as part of the learning cycle. Criteria are developed at the outset of establishing the learning plan. These criteria are revised as the learner gains deeper understanding of the needs she or he wants to achieve. The questions used to develop criteria include:

- How will I know when I have met my learning objectives?
- Why do I see these objectives as important?
- What reasons can I offer for the choices I have made to meet my learning needs? (ibid.: 92)

Criteria offered by external bodies for accreditation purposes can also be incorporated. The mentor's role is to help the learner set rigorous criteria for assessment and evaluation of the quality of the learning that can be judged by the type of criteria set and the learning outcomes themselves. Rigorous self-assessment and evaluation of the process and outcomes, facilitated by the mentor, is essential for the learner in the development of the professional skills of self-assessment and evaluation of learning.

In nursing and the medical profession 'portfolio learning' has encouraged reflective learner-centred approaches to learning for professionals. Snadden and Thomas (1998: 192) define portfolio learning as 'documentation of learning and articulation of what has been learned'. It is suggested that the documentation in this field can include:

- records of events or experiences;
- lists of critical reviews or articles read;
- projects carried out;
- teaching sessions attended; and
- video clips, educational events and patients seen.

Suggested examples of articulation of what has been learned are:

- written reflective accounts of the events documented; and
- personal reflections kept in the form of a journal or diary of problem areas, learning outcomes and action plans for future learning.

The use of the portfolio in the medical profession is a means of facilitating professional growth. The documentation and articulation of the learning is used to stimulate substantive discussion between the learner and supervisor. The supervisor's role in the discussion is to guide further learning by helping to focus the learner on their experiences and clinical practice and to draw out learning points. The learner provides evidence in the portfolio to demonstrate that learning has taken place. Snadden and Thomas (1998: 194) suggest the following types of evidence for inclusion in the portfolio:

- critical incidents of events with patients;
- a reflective journal or diary;
- tutorials and learning plans, reflection on them;
- routine clinical experiences;
- exam preparation material;
- video-recordings of consultations and other relevant material;
- audits and project work;
- critical reviews of articles;
- feedback material; and
- management material.

This evidence provides a written record of what has been accomplished in a training period, a record of learning needs and how these were met and an individual curriculum that fits the needs and experience of the doctor or student. Snadden and Thomas (1998) acknowledge these benefits of portfolio use in medical education but emphasise that the issue of assessing the portfolio remains a dilemma. The reasons for this relate to the traditional, quantitative conceptions of assessment and the prevailing assessment paradigm that is not supportive of more personalised and individual curriculum. They conclude that while the emphasis on grading, excellence and comparison between students and doctors remains in assessment and medicine the portfolio will serve more of a learning function than a summative assessment tool. It has been argued in this book that tensions will emerge when the portfolio is used for a different purpose other than that for which it was intended.

Developing a portfolio for assessment and learning purposes in the context of teacher education has been discussed throughout this book; more recently it has emerged as a significant feature in ongoing and continuing professional development. For example, in the Post Graduate Certificate in Education (PGCE) history course at the Institute of Education, University of London, students are encouraged to maintain a professional portfolio to provide documentation and support that will help them manage their own career path in teaching. The portfolio reflects the individual as teacher and professional. It incorporates individual experiences, focus and areas of specialism and achievement. These students are informed that the portfolio is 'a unique profile that can reflect not just . . . achievements but also . . . development and progress' (Ashby, 1998). The construction of a portfolio is seen as an example of the individual being pro-active in demonstrating her or his achievements. Suggested examples of sections to be included are:

- philosophical statement of the kind of teacher you are aiming to be and what you feel constitutes a good teacher;

- a statement about the value of the history to pupils' education and its relevance to the world in which they live;
- a *curriculum vitae* that includes your education and qualifications, extended as you go to include a section on professional development sessions and courses you have attended, new qualifications that you may gain;
- a statement of historical content of your degree course, additional curriculum knowledge that you may have acquired, new reading that you have undertaken;
- a record of examination syllabuses you have taught, both General Certificate of Secondary Education and A Level, and any additional subjects that you have some experience in teaching;
- a statement of your Information Computing and Technology (ICT) capability and teaching experience;
- a research record;
- examples of resources you have developed for use in the classroom;
- examples of lesson plans and evaluations that have provided you with key learning experiences;
- extracts from observation reports about your subject knowledge, planning, teaching, class management and assessment and recording of pupil work;
- extracts about your approach to pupils, colleagues, parents; and
- extracts from reports that identify particular achievements or abilities (Ashby, 1998).

It is this type of portfolio of work that individuals can use to demonstrate achievements at interviews or for appraisal purposes. Record of achievements, education and experiences support individual's analyses of their abilities and supplies others with relevant information for judging the individual's suitability for positions of responsibilities and career opportunities. In addition, for teachers the portfolio of work provides an opportunity for the teacher to reflect on her or his expectations of student work and the types of classroom experiences encountered.

A longitudinal benefit of a portfolio of work for an individual is that it allows the opportunity to examine approaches to learning as well as strengths and areas in need of improvement. In reviewing work over time an individual can evaluate how thinking and learning strategies and processes have improved.

Insights into complex learning experiences are possible when curriculum and assessment are integrated. Portfolios allow for the assessment of:

- development in physical and emotional skills;
- cognitive skills as reflected in course work or individualised curriculum as documented over time;
- group work such as cooperation and social skills;
- growth in a range of academic subject areas;
- learning processes and quality of thinking through self-evaluations and reflective statements; and
- progression in learning such as plans, drafts of work, final products.

Principles

Research conducted on the use of portfolios for assessment and learning purposes in the context of teacher education and a review of current literature about the use of portfolios across the professions led to the identification of six principles that underpin this practice. The first principle relates to the focus on learning and the impact on cognitive and affective development. The integration of learning with assessment is emphasised. The second principle is linked to the developmental nature of the portfolio. Issues related to growth, and development in scope are explained. The documentation of process artefacts is a unique feature of portfolio use. Achievements can be analysed and evaluated and such analyses of learning experiences form the third principle. Self-evaluation is integral to portfolio use and this fourth principle has been emphasised. The process of reflecting on one's learning styles and developing metacognitive awareness through portfolio use is described. The processes of collecting work then selecting evidence from this collection and reflecting on the examples of work for the portfolio relates to the fifth principle. The role of the teacher as facilitator of learning is associated with the sixth principle included in the discussion.

New perspective on learning

The use of portfolios for assessment purposes provides a new perspective on learning. In developing a portfolio of work, students are engaged in learning as an interactive process. The portfolio connects process and product. Student learning is documented and the expectation is that they will actively explore and evaluate that learning through engaging with their teachers, other students or peers. Collaboration, dialogue and reflection become essential processes in the construction of the portfolio of work.

Pupils' views of successful learning activities according to research carried out by Flutter *et al.* (1999: 36–7) are those that:

- provide opportunities to be creative and inventive;
- incorporate novelty and challenge;
- offer choice and a sense of ownership; and
- raise awareness of progress.

These qualities are inherent in the portfolio assessment processes because the individual owns the portfolio and is responsible for organising and selecting the work to be included. When students manage their own portfolios they are developing important organising skills which help in extending their responsibility and ownership of their work. Creativity and the opportunity to be inventive exist as students strive to develop a portfolio of work that captures their unique, personal achievements. Creativity and independence in learning are encouraged. The portfolio shifts the agency from the teacher to the student. This contrasts with other forms of assessment where the teacher is in charge of processes and assessment is a technical act that is focused exclusively on what the student can do. The student in portfolio assessment is actively engaged in thinking about his or her own work, learning and the progress he or she is making.

Students' initial reactions of anxiety and uncertainty about the portfolio processes and their limited experience in setting standards for their own progress and achievement have been documented (Hootstein, 1999). Students need multiple opportunities to analyse, self-evaluate and reflect on their own learning experiences. These processes help to personalise the learning for students as they develop increased understanding and confidence with the portfolio processes. Learning becomes grounded in their experiences.

When students document their learning outcomes, and the learning processes involved, they provide essential information for teachers to evaluate more accurately what they know, can and cannot do, compared to reductionist assessment strategies. Teachers can monitor the complexity of an activity as the students are engaged with it and as they are developing understanding and skills.

The use of a portfolio for learning and assessment allows the learners to assume responsibility for their own personal and professional development. The learner assumes responsibility for planning, managing and evaluating the learning. There is also flexibility in the portfolio process for learners to work at their own pace and style. The learners' strengths and learning needs are made more apparent and self-direction and autonomy are fostered.

Developmental process

The second principle is that portfolio assessment is a developmental process. The focus is on student growth in curriculum areas over time (e.g. skills in literacy, mathematical problem-solving, cognitive development). Students demonstrate growth through appropriate selection of work samples. For pre-service teachers this includes materials to illustrate concepts of teaching and learning that underpin their work and documentation of student learning. Video-segments that illustrate growth in skills such as teaching, questioning, presenting or managing the learning environment can be included in the portfolio as evidence.

Chronologically sequencing students' work and recording the development, 'macro-genesis' (long-term evolution) provides a powerful insight into the students' learning process (Cole *et al.*, 2000: 16). Portfolios can be structured to document successes and failures to encourage dialogue and analysis to promote deep learning.

When the design of the assessment of the portfolio is developmental, specific curriculum fields are integrated with assessment. The use of developmental continua allows students to take ownership of their progress in learning. An example is given in chapter 3 of the spelling developmental continua from the 'First Steps' literacy programme of the Education Department of Western Australia. Teachers, and students themselves, are able to monitor growth according to these developmental phases where the focus is on the learning rather than grade or age-level indicators. For today's learners to be self-determining it is necessary to self-monitor and self-evaluate.

While the dynamic, developmental nature of the portfolio may not be apparent for the purpose of demonstrating 'best work' in a showcase portfolio (Forster and Masters, 1996) the developmental process remains essential in its construction. Learning is ongoing and reflection is the tool for presenting the work most effectively (Wyatt III and Looper, 1999).

Analyses of achievements and learning

Another principle relates to the documentation of achievements, and analyses of learning. The documentation can include evaluations of work by self, peers or supervisors, analyses of learning and teaching practices facilitated by substantive dialogue with others. In analysing the work to be included in the portfolio the student is attaching meaning to that work. The process of verbalising and writing about the work selected for the collection in the portfolio is powerful in promoting metacognitive growth and self-awareness (Bailey and Guskey, 2001).

The strength of portfolio use derives from this process – the learning and the sense of accomplishment. Students can benefit from analyses of their learning by engaging in dialogue that promotes new understandings by:

- sensitising existing constructions through personal awareness;
- analysing them consciously;
- soliciting conflicting perspectives; and
- resolving the conflicts into new, better-informed constructions (Jarvinen and Kohonen, 1995: 29).

Giving students opportunities to examine and to carry out analyses of their ideas, beliefs, constructions and values in collaboration with others supports this process and develops increased awareness of their learning. Students are focusing their attention on the process of learning and in so doing making progress in their learning to achieve desired learning outcomes. The emphasis here is on the process or the means to achieve the ends rather than a focus on the ends in themselves. Including analyses of learning in the portfolio provides an insight for the teacher into how and why students choose particular courses of action. The focus shifts from an evaluation of what students can do to a consideration of why they choose particular strategies or approaches to their learning. For students to assume this responsibility in the learning process they need to be actively engaged in managing their own learning and see the relevance and value of the work accomplished.

In teacher education when pre-service teachers develop the practice of documenting and analysing their teaching and engage in meaningful conversations with their colleagues about their practice, they are developing their own values and philosophies about teaching which will help to build a culture that values reflective, collaborative practice. This is a quality valued in teaching.

Self-evaluation

The fourth principle is that self-evaluation is an integral process of portfolio use. Claxton (1999) promotes the view that the learner has to be his or her own 'learning coach'. He explains:

> You have to be able to monitor your own progress; if necessary even to measure it; to mull over different options and courses of development; to be mindful of your own assumptions and habits, and able to stand back from them and appraise them when learning gets stuck; and in general manage yourself as a learner – prioritizing, planning, reviewing progress, revising strategy and if necessary changing tack . . . Good learners need to assume the ability to evaluate their own progress: to tell for themselves when they have done 'good' work.
>
> (1999: 14)

To understand this level of self-knowledge teachers need to encourage students to self-evaluate past and present work. It is important for students to realise what they do and do not understand about a given subject (Bailey and Guskey, 2001). Students come to know more about themselves and the thinking that develops their learning by engaging in self-evaluations of their work and learning. The portfolio that requires the student to document work over time allows them to see learning as a process that is shaped by diverse experiences and contexts (Freidus, 1998: 62).

From the research it is apparent that students find it difficult to self-evaluate; this is why it is important to teach the language of evaluation. Students need to understand the concept of criteria and have some experience in developing them. This will help them to understand the criteria developed by teachers or others. Teacher feedback and peer review are important practices to help students develop the skills of self-evaluation. Students are able to develop more meaningful self-evaluative comments with this type of assistance. Developing this skill is helpful in working towards increased reflectivity.

A portfolio assessment system requires the student to take responsibility to record, to engage metacognitively and to reflect on their learning of knowledge, skills and attitudes. Performance assessment, an integral aspect of portfolio assessment, shifts the responsibility to the students to demonstrate what they know and can do rather than being required to state what it is they know and can do or to be questioned about it.

From the outset students need to understand their responsibility for self-learning and commitment to developing and maintaining a portfolio of work. They also need to know that they are expected to be thoughtful about the selection of work for inclusion and that they need to develop a reflective capacity. Such learning characteristics and habits of mind help to foster further learning.

When students evaluate and respond thoughtfully to their own work they develop metacognitively – the ability to think about their thinking. They are expected to evaluate the learning outcomes and the processes used to achieve such learning. This documentation of the student's learning is important in providing a history of the student's learning and can facilitate independence in learning and self-actualisation. Nitko (1998) has indicated that metacognitive development can be assessed by interviewing students or asking students to explain their thinking, planning or monitoring of their progress. As has been argued the portfolio allows students to include analyses of these dimensions in relation to the work included.

Student choice and reflection on work

Students need to have decision-making power about which work is chosen for inclusion in the portfolio if they are to feel ownership of the process and the portfolio. The student is responsible for collating and developing the work for the portfolio and should be given some opportunity to choose and reflect on the work to be used in demonstrating achievement. When students create the work for the portfolio it is helpful if they are aware that the work selected and included is a representation of their efforts and accomplishments. Their understanding of the criteria and standards for the assessment of their learning becomes important in this endeavour.

The Learning Record used to assess literacy is a standards-referenced system that produces detailed and summary information about how students are performing (Barr *et al.*, 1999). The standards are externally formulated and are accessible to both the teacher and the learner. The student sees examples of what the standards imply and can work with the teacher to improve performance. Sadler (quoted in Barr *et al.*, 1999: 11) argues that 'collecting evidence is not in itself enough. The evidence must be sifted, understood and related to a scale of performance'. He goes on to suggest that students 'need to develop the ability to make reasoned judgements about the quality of their work' so that they can manage the quality of their own work while they are actually producing it. This assists the learner in developing autonomous learning skills and to assume greater responsibility for his or her own learning. Such outcomes are achieved by giving learners the opportunity to make judgements about work of the same quality they are attempting to produce themselves. The selection of work for the portfolio provides the learner with these important experiences.

Portfolios contain process artefacts demonstrating student progress and their reflections on selected evidence and on their learning. Reflections, which involve analysis of learning and self-development, also help students develop responsibility for learning and demonstrate intended learning outcomes – i.e. engagement with the curriculum. The students' reflections on their own learning characteristics, values and beliefs will make these aspects more explicit in the portfolio of work. Encouraging the student to reflect on the learning experience will also help and enhance learning itself. This is because portfolios provide opportunities for reflection on experience and problem-solving which involve cycles of thought, action and reflection.

Developing the capacity to select evidence to show attainment of particular competencies takes time and skills in evaluation. Feedback to the student is helpful in the development of skills to address these processes. Providing the opportunity for students to develop a critical reflective capacity is fundamental to the portfolio process. Instead of accepting the judgement, values, ideas, philosophy of others, students with suitable support and teaching can develop a critical and reflective attitude towards ideas. Paul (1990) indicates that as we reflect and integrate the insights we discover, our beliefs become more our own creation rather than the absorption of the beliefs of others. Paul warns that if we provide teachers with exercises for their students that simply promote technical competence in thinking, and if the thinking of teachers is not challenged, they will inadvertently pass on their own deep-seated prejudices to their students. Teachers will assume that their thinking is adequate rather than seriously question whether it is sensitive to 'root ideas, to alternative frames of reference and to the logic of what is said'. He concludes: '. . . thinking of teachers is deeply involved at every level of teaching. Left unreformed by self-analysis and critique, little will change in the students' thoughts' (ibid.: 474).

Teachers need to understand reflection and be reflective themselves to guide their students. Reflections involve analysis and synthesis of knowledge, skills, and attitudes as they develop. The following types of questions help to structure reflections.

Reflective Entry Questions (Cole *et al.*, 2000: 16):
- Why is this your best work?
- How did you go about accomplishing this task?
- What would you do differently if you did a task like this again?
- Where do you go from here?

Further questions to assist students and professionals to reflect on their work have been collated by Arter and Spandel (1992: 40). These include:

- Describe the process you went through to complete this assignment. Include where you got ideas, how you explored the subject, what problems you encountered, and what revision strategies you used.
- List the points made by the group review of your work. Describe your response to each point – did you agree or disagree? Why? What did you do as the result of your feedback?
- What makes your most effective piece different from your least effective piece?
- How does this activity relate to what you have learned before?
- What are the strengths of your work? What still makes you uneasy?

Teacher's facilitative role

Curriculum, assessment and pedagogy intersect via the use of portfolios for assessment and learning purposes. This is possible if the teacher assumes a facilitative role in the learning process and views assessment as integral to the teaching and learning cycle. The teacher's role as facilitator is to encourage the learners to develop their own strategies and discover their own solutions. The teacher as facilitator also helps the students to reflect critically on their learning experiences and to explore different perspectives.

In implementing portfolios the teacher's role is fundamental in preparing and managing the learning environment. Time, guidance, feedback and support are necessary for students to develop confidence, independence and ownership of the learning processes involved in developing a portfolio of work. While students are engaged in producing the portfolio of work, teachers observe, listen, discuss, question and intervene to help extend student learning experiences. Through such engagement teachers develop understanding and insights into the knowledge and skills of their students. It is crucial that the teacher knows what a student can do independently and what the student can do with varying levels of assistance. Teachers also need to be aware of how students use their help and what forms of assistance prove most useful to learning.

From their knowledge and teaching experience, teachers are aware that students use different learning styles, take varying amounts of time to integrate learning and learn at varying levels. Teachers also develop methods of evaluating, monitoring and recording individual student growth. This involves finding evidence of improvement, effort, reflection, risk-taking and change in the student's learning. Teachers during these processes are providing feedback that is transformative in facilitating student learning and in guiding reflectivity.

What the portfolio should include and reasons for incorporating this work into the portfolio needs to be negotiated, discussed and made apparent to the students. This involves identification of the curriculum aims and standards, clarification of the pedagogical principles and assessment strategies to be used to achieve these curriculum goals. The assessment of the learning is designed developmentally. This requires a clear understanding of expectations and criteria. Teachers need to be clear about what work provides evidence of the intended learning outcomes. They need to be able to guide students in the selection of work that will help illustrate growth and development. This allows students to benefit from examining their work that reflects such growth and illustrates their strengths as well as the areas in need of improvement. Research suggests that students like to become involved in collaborative assessment with the teacher, and this experience impacts positively on learning itself and the learner's attitude about learning (Sadler in Barr *et al.*, 1999).

The teacher's role as facilitator can be demonstrated in the context of the substantive dialogue that takes place between the learner and the teacher or mentor in the development of work for the portfolio. In the dialogue about the learning, the student describes, firstly, the experience which includes the feelings and reactions without analysis at this stage. The teacher then encourages the student to evaluate the experience. To make sense of that experience, analysis is also needed. Conclusions are reached from the experience and the analysis and implications for action are identified to make the most of what has been learnt. The plan of action developed from such evaluation and analysis should include learning objectives, resources and strategies with an indication of how that learning will be achieved and assessed (Pietroni and Millard, 1997).

Desired curriculum outcomes of higher order thinking require the integration by students of their learning in realistic applications. The implications for pedagogic practices are numerous. Students need to assess, evaluate, manage, organise and use information for problem-solving, decision-making and critical thinking in the development of the portfolio of work. The teacher's role as a facilitator becomes vital.

Summary

- Portfolios are being used increasingly for professional preparation, appraisal and career advancement, in medical and teacher education.
- In medical education the learner-centred nature of the portfolio allows the individual to develop a professional development programme to meet their particular needs identified through critical incidents or case analysis.
- Portfolios allow for the assessment of skills that are physical, emotional or cognitive and growth in learning processes and quality of thinking.
- Six principles that underpin the use of portfolios include: promotes a new perspective on learning, is a developmental process, incorporates analyses of achievements and learning, requires self-evaluation, encourages student choice and reflection on work, engages teachers or mentors as facilitators of learning.

7 Portfolios and changes in assessment

This chapter analyses the reasons for the increasing dissatisfaction with traditional, quantitative forms of assessment, which has led to the development of alternative assessment approaches that include the use of the portfolio. The argument developed is based on the belief that the use of portfolios for both assessment and learning purposes provides opportunities for demonstrating learning and for supporting the development of important learning dispositions, processes and strategies. The reasons for using a portfolio of work to assess and support learning in terms of constructivist learning theory and Vygotsky's notion of the zone of proximal development are given. The alignment of portfolio use with constructivist learning theory has implications for a pedagogy that supports the development of important skills. As illustrated in chapters 2 and 6, how this learning theory that underpins portfolio use gets translated into practice is exemplified in the context of teacher and medical education.

Dissatisfaction with quantitative approaches

The last decade of the twentieth century saw increased international dissatisfaction with the more quantitative, traditional forms of assessment (Gipps, 1994; Biggs, 1996; Gardner, 1992; Wiggins, 1989). Much of this aversion stemmed from the view of learning on which these assessments were designed and their impacts on teaching and learning. Assessment approaches from this quantitative tradition have been challenged and alternative approaches, such as the portfolio, have emerged.

Portfolio use for assessment purposes parallels the shift from a quantitative tradition of assessment to a more qualitative approach (Biggs, 1996). Factors that have contributed to this move include changing theories of learning and their associated impact on curriculum and pedagogy to promote active student engagement with learning.

In the quantitative tradition, curriculum is viewed as discrete units, listed as decontextualised objectives and possibly including facts, skills, competencies, behavioural objectives or performance indicators. The teacher transmits units of knowledge to students in a fixed time frame. The learner follows a predetermined course and attempts to acquire the content transmitted by the teacher. The teacher's feedback on the learner's performance is delayed and assessment is norm-referenced. That is, the individual's result is relative to the performance of others and the focus is on the measurement of how much has been attained (Griffin, 1998a).

Tests developed within this tradition usually require the aggregation of item scores (as in multiple-choice tests) and essay marks (sum total of marks for each acceptable point made). But it has been argued that this method of assessment gives students false messages about the structure of knowledge (Biggs, 1996). Such assessment practices atomise knowledge. A common student response is to focus on exam technique rather than learning with understanding. Tests developed based on such quantitative assumptions do not allow for an indication of the full range of learning outcomes attained.

It is not surprising that traditional forms of assessment are disfavoured. For some time now, many educators (Gardner, 1992; Resnick and Resnick, 1992; Gifford and O'Connor, 1994; Gipps, 1994; Biggs, 1996) have indicated the need for better approaches to be implemented. For example, Shepard (2000) observes that traditional views of testing continue to impinge on curriculum and pedagogy with the result that outdated ideas continue to shape the curriculum, instruction practices and policies of today.

Assessment practice in the United States has been characterised by standardised tests; (Perrone, 1991, Sacks, 1999). Sacks (ibid.: 256) notes that: '[t]he adults' test-driven classrooms exacerbate boredom, fear, and lethargy promoting all manner of mechanical behaviours on the part of teachers, students, and schools, and bleed schoolchildren of their natural love of learning'. In these contexts student assessment is characterised by a bureaucratic evaluation system that values the measurement of learning for accountability purposes and is inimical to what Resnick and Resnick (1992) have called the 'thinking curriculum'. In England a test-driven curriculum has evolved without significant attention to teachers' assessments of student progress through portfolios, presentations or authentic tasks. While many teachers believe in active student engagement in setting, monitoring and internalising standards, the pressure for national testing of student performance has constrained the practice of self-evaluation, negotiating grades, group work and collaborative learning (Lofty, 1993). In their efforts to raise standards through national curriculum testing, league tables of school performance, target-setting and inspections of schools, governments in the Deweyian sense are not 'hitting the target'. This culture of accountability driven by a focus on targets and standards has diminished both teacher and student agency. Increasingly teachers are told what to teach and how to teach. Take, for example, the implementation in England and Wales of the literacy and numeracy initiatives. More recently the Qualifications and Curriculum Authority (QCA) has developed schemes of work, for every subject of the General Certificate of Secondary Education (GCSE). It is likely that inspectors will now be inspecting teaching to assess whether teachers are implementing these schemes of work faithfully.

Black and Wiliam (1998) in their extensive review of research about formative assessment concluded that researchers internationally have found that external tests such as the General Certificate of Secondary Education tests (GCSEs) inevitably dominate both teaching and assessment. The results of such tests are used to provide overall summaries of achievement rather than to analyse learning and to provide important formative feedback for improvement purposes.

In England, in 1998, the higher education minister critiqued the main school exam, the traditional A-Level, in which students typically take two or three subjects. She described the system as '. . . "wrong": too narrow, too specialised, too elitist, and "designed for a world that no longer exists"' (Targett, 1998: vii). Evidence of further dissatisfaction with traditional forms of assessment.

In Hong Kong, examinations have hindered students achieving personal understandings of subject. The emphasis on testing for selection has resulted in backwash that dominates teaching and learning throughout the primary and secondary school sectors. Teachers second-guess the examinations and provide notes, model answers and opportunities for students to recall the given information. This reduces learning to the lowest cognitive level (Biggs, 1996).

At the heart of the dissatisfaction with conventional forms of assessment is the use of school-leaving examinations for purposes of selection. A single indicator of achievement as a basis for making significant decisions is questionable. A major criticism of traditional examinations is their concentration on the evaluation of the 'product' rather than of the 'process' of learning. Product refers to the outcomes, the conclusions, findings, facts, information, discoveries or disclosures of learning. Process refers to the methods, procedures, habits of thinking, techniques, strategies or skills involved in problem-solving, establishing the relevant facts or determining the relevant conclusions (Williams, 1992). The quantitative, reductionist forms of assessment depend on a norm-based system that evaluates every student in relation to the norms of achievement of others doing the same examination. A proportion of students will therefore inevitably fail. Internationally there has been a theoretical shift from norm-referenced to criterion-referenced assessment systems and a corresponding move towards more qualitative assessment approaches.

A further argument advanced by critics to indicate their dissatisfaction with traditional forms of assessment relates to the nature of some tests. It has been argued that some tests make the complex simple. This occurs when the learning to be tested is broken down into isolated and simplistic tasks that do not require the student to consider the problem holistically and to practise problem-solving by working with all the elements. This approach of deconstructing tasks leads to tests that assess artificially isolated 'outcomes' that do not promote genuine intellectual endeavour. It encourages teaching to the test (Wiggins, 1989) and fosters mechanical and disengaging pedagogy. This decomposability assumption has been seriously challenged by cognitive research. Resnick and Resnick (1992) have argued that complex competencies cannot be defined by listing all of their components. Trying to assess thinking and problem-solving abilities by separating components and then testing them independently interferes with effective teaching of such skills and does not encourage real problem-solving or interpretive thinking. The effect of context on performance is important. A skill component taught in one context cannot be applied automatically in another and a competency cannot validly be assessed in a context that differs greatly to that in which it is practised or used. The implication is to provide the most appropriate contexts in which to assess competencies. The major criticisms of quantitative approaches to assessment are as follows:

- teachers teach to the test;
- external assessments for accountability purposes impact detrimentally on pedagogy and inhibit educational assessment;
- tests drive and narrow the curriculum;
- standardised tests assess lower-level thinking skills to the neglect of higher-level thinking and learning skills (Lieberman, 1991; Darling-Hammond, 1991);
- emphasis on test results and standards focus on products and academic purposes to the detriment of the social, affective and physical educational purposes (Suarez and Gottovi, 1992);
- summative test results provide teachers with inadequate information for teaching purposes; and
- meaningful feedback for student development is lacking.

Alternative approaches to assessment

Alternative assessment methods have emerged in response to the dissatisfaction with quantitative systems. A catalyst for such change has also been the realisation that the type of assessment impacts profoundly on learning dispositions, attitudes, strategies adopted and learning ability (Broadfoot, 1996). Developments in both learning theories and the theory of educational assessment (Gipps, 1994) have supported the move towards authentic, alternative assessments, such as the portfolio. For example, constructivist views of learning and more qualitative approaches to assessment are central to the use of portfolios.

The conceptualisation of multiple intelligences (Gardner, 1983) – verbal-linguistic; logical-mathematical; visual-spatial representation; musical-rhythmic analysis; bodily-kinesthetic thinking and two forms of personal understanding (interpersonal knowledge and intrapersonal knowledge) – led to the call for 'intelligence-fair' assessment (Gardner, 1992). To illustrate this point, in the United States it has been claimed that formal testing evaluates primarily the verbal-linguistic and logical-mathematical to the neglect of other intelligences. Alternative assessments for learning suggested by Gardner (ibid.) incorporate regular reflection on learning and teaching goals, the means to achieve them, the extent to which these goals have been achieved and the implications for rethinking goals or procedures. He advocates methods and measures that aid in the regular, systematic and useful assessment of learning within the natural learning environment.

Critique of the utility of tests in measuring what students actually know inspired a move towards 'alternative, authentic assessment' approaches (Wiggins, 1989, 1991; Newmann, 1991; Harnisch and Mabry, 1993; Brandt, 1992; Zessoules and Gardner, 1991). Authentic assessment includes tasks that challenge the individual's intellect and test intellectual ability in a manner which reflects probable experience for the individual in the field (Wiggins, 1989). The principles that underpin authentic assessment have been identified by Cormack *et al.* (1998) and are summarised as follows:

- connects to the curriculum;
- engages students, teachers and others in assessing performance;
- looks beyond the school for models and sites of action;
- promotes complex thinking and problem-solving;
- encourages student 'performance' of their learning; and
- engages with issues of equity.

Alternative authentic assessments are varied and comprehensive encouraging multiple methods for demonstrating learning. They have a broader conceptualisation of what a test is (Wiggins, 1989). Problem-solving in this assessment context requires students to think analytically and demonstrate their proficiency, as they would in situations beyond the classroom (Archbald and Newmann, 1988). As indicated by Cormack *et al.* (1998) authentic assessment can promote learning opportunities beyond the classroom, in out of school sites, that encourage students to develop skills, understandings and insights relevant to their particular needs and contexts. Standardised tests fail to examine skills required for the solution of real-life – social, political or scientific – problems. Assessments for learning require an understanding of the different intelligences and diverse cognitive styles of individuals. Gardner (1992) has also argued for an awareness of the qualities that are characteristic of creative individuals in different domains.

A further purpose of new approaches is to make assessment fairer by reducing the dependence on performance in a single terminal examination as the only determinant of student achievement and by giving individuals the opportunity to demonstrate attainment over time and in a variety of contexts. Another aim is to make assessment more accurate and reflective of an individual's learning and development by identifying the abilities being examined. This helps to encompass a wider range of abilities and facilitates the recording of achievement.

The use of teacher- or school-based assessment is another alternative, for it is in this context that locally developed indicators can prove to be more effective educationally than examinations or tests administered from the centre. One testing method does not fit all circumstances. Multiple judges are recommended (Wiggins, 1991). In the Australian state of Queensland, students' work is assessed at the local level and forms part of the state system of assessment of student performance (Maxwell and Cumming, 1998). Data are collected both formally and informally and used by teachers and administrators to set learning goals and priorities to build on what students already know. Standard-setting and assessment are linked when teachers design assessments that are intellectually challenging for their students. Teachers set standards as they identify the actual tasks that they want students to be good at and they provide various opportunities for students to display thoughtful control over ideas (Wiggins, 1989).

Curriculum design, assessment and learning are integral processes, and teachers should provide opportunities for students to develop learning strategies essential for future learning rather than view them simply as measures of achievement. Skills and knowledge of a domain should be viewed as 'enabling competencies for the future' (Glaser, 1990: 480). That is to say, knowledge should be assessed in terms of its constructive use for further learning. The implication is that assessments should promote the competencies for success in either, or both, the academic disciplines or the workplace. Students need to be challenged and given the opportunity to develop standards and habits both to succeed and to continue learning.

Portfolios used for the assessment of student learning offer an opportunity to redress some of the limitations of reductionist assessment procedures and represent an alternative approach that is underpinned by constructivist views of learning. Current theories of learning advocate active student engagement in learning and assessment, together with ongoing interaction between teacher and student in order to improve the quality of learning and the construction of meaning. There are implications here for pedagogical practices and curriculum design. These implications are now explored by analysing how the use of portfolios for assessment aligns with constructivist learning theory.

Alignment with constructivist learning theory

Any discussion of the use of portfolios for assessment practice must be grounded in a broader framework of learning theory, for assessment is integral to the learning and teaching cycle (Glaser, 1990; Stiggins, 1992; McClure and Walters, 1992; Broadfoot, 1996; Harlen and James, 1997; Black and Wiliam, 1998; Hattie and Jaeger, 1998).

In the United States, Shepard (2000) has developed a historical framework that illustrates clearly how changing conceptions of curriculum, learning theory and measurement demonstrate how traditional, measurement views of testing hinder the implementation of constructivist views of learning and teaching. In the framework constructed, she shows how the dominant paradigm in the twentieth century was influenced by a curriculum theory derived from notions of social efficiency and scientific management. It linked closely with hereditarian theories of intelligence and with associationist and behaviorist theories of learning. She explains that these psychological theories were aligned to and served by an aspiration to the scientific measurement of ability and achievement. What becomes apparent from Shepard's analysis of curriculum, psychological and measurement theories of the last century is their profound impact on the conceptualisation of subject matter and consequences for pedagogy and assessment. As she states: 'One hundred years ago, various recall, completion, matching, and multiple-choice test types fit[ted] closely with what was deemed important to learn' (ibid.: 7).

Just as there have been changes in our understanding and design of curriculum and assessment, so too have there been changes in the way we understand how learning takes place. Epistemologically the shift is from a static, passive view of knowledge transmission to a more active view of knowledge construction that is seen as an interactive, organic process of reorganisation and restructuring by the learner (Gipps, 1998b; Murphy, 1997). Constructivist views of learning see the learner as an active interpreter and constructor of knowledge based on experiences and interactions with the environment.

This more qualitative view of learning emphasises the learner's active engagement in making sense of new knowledge and in deciding how to integrate it with previously held concepts and information. This contrasts with the view that knowledge is stable and learning involves the recall of facts. Assessment in the qualitative tradition is complex and requires the teacher to analyse the learning strategies the student uses. The nature of learning (active interpretation and construction of knowledge) is fundamental in this constructivist paradigm.

Learning is viewed as a cumulative process. The teacher's task is to help students construct meaning that aligns with accepted constructs. Students will only change their beliefs when these ideas are no longer effective or another alternative seems preferable. Teachers form a model of the students' ways of viewing an idea then assist the student in restructuring those views so that they become more adequate from both the students' and the teacher's perspective (Confrey, 1990). Students' constructions can of course differ from those of the teacher. They should therefore be encouraged to express their beliefs so that the teacher comes to understand them. Indeed the teacher may need to revise his or her own beliefs or to negotiate with the student to find a mutually acceptable alternative. There is interpretation and knowledge construction on the part of the student. The teacher intervenes in this ongoing process of knowledge construction providing students with opportunities to develop their learning and metacognitive skills. Learning is not a simple recording of information. Teachers and students work together in the knowledge-construction process.

Guba and Lincoln (1989) define the constructivist paradigm as a series of mental constructions that require interactivity for construction or subsequent reconstruction. The 'hermeneutic methodology' (Guba and Lincoln, 1989) used during this interaction and joint construction involves processes of iteration, analysis, critique, reiteration and reanalysis. Opportunities to exhibit or demonstrate learning and to peer or self-evaluate learning are required. When these process artefacts of reflective commentaries are included as evidence in the portfolio, and discussed, the opportunity exists for students to reconstruct or jointly construct meaning during teacher–student or student–student interactions centred on the portfolio of work.

Vygotsky's theory is also useful in this context of assessment that both reflects and supports learning. The processes described above are consistent with his theory that the development of cognitive processes is a highly interactive, social experience. Shepard (1992) suggests that Vygotsky developed assessment techniques based on focused intervention so teachers could learn by thinking about how students had responded to teaching. Focused intervention thus relates to Vygotsky's zone of proximal development (zpd).

The zone of proximal development has been described by Tharp and Gallimore (1988) as the development of a cognitive skill that an individual has only partially mastered but can be used successfully and internalised with the assistance and supervision of someone more experienced. This distance between the child's individual capacity and the capacity to perform with assistance is described further as:

> the distance between the actual developmental level as determined by individual problem solving and the level of potential development as determined through problem solving under adult guidance or in collaboration with more capable peers

(ibid.: 30)

Tharp and Gallimore (1998) refer to Vygotsky's (1978) notion of zpd as defining functions that are in the process of maturation or analogous to 'buds' or 'flowers' rather than the 'fruits' of development. It is suggested that there is no single zone for each individual but rather for any domain of skill a zpd can be developed. Cultural zones as well as individual zones are mentioned because of the cultural variations in competencies that students acquire through social interaction in a particular society.

From this perspective the most effective social interaction to facilitate cognitive development is joint problem-solving in the zone of proximal development with guidance given by someone who is more skilled. This is similar to an apprenticeship model of learning where a novice works closely with an expert in joint problem-solving. The expert guides the novice in trying skills that would otherwise remain beyond his or her capability. The novice's existing knowledge and skills develop as the shared cognitive processes, and the skills carried out in collaboration are internalised (Rogoff, 1999).

When the teacher or more capable other provides assistance, internal developmental processes are activated and when these are internalised they form part of the child's independent developmental achievement. Teaching is considered effective when 'it *awakens* and rouses to life those functions which are in a stage of maturing, which lie in the zone of proximal development' (ibid.: 31). Four stages of zpd are outlined by Tharp and Gallimore.[1]

In this theory of learning interaction is considered the means by which children begin to use the intellectual tools of their society and therefore the partner must know more about these tools than the child. Vygotsky's theory of zpd led Bruner (1986) to define areas beyond an individual's generative competence, that is where an individual could follow someone else's thoughts and actions without being able to construct them personally. The interaction between one's own reflective understanding and that of the teacher assist an individual to transform and develop personal consciousness to a more comprehensive level of organisation. The importance of self and self-reflection are emphasised.

The significance of engaging students in the processes of developing a portfolio of work is best understood in the context of this conception of learning. Teachers are able to promote student learning when they provide feedback that supports and impacts on learning. In the portfolio process this occurs when the students collect, select and evaluate their own work. They discuss with their teachers their exhibitions and evaluations of learning and make a plan for future action. 'One does not have to wait until a child is developmentally ready before beginning instruction' (Rosenshine and Meister, 1994: 483). In Vygotsky's own words, 'what the child is able to do in collaboration today, he [or she] will be able to do independently tomorrow' (Rieber and Carton, 1987: 211). Teaching must lead development forward (Vygotsky quoted in Davydov, 1995).

The impact of theories of guided learning are thus evident in practices such as scaffolding and reciprocal teaching both, of which have important implications for the development of a portfolio of work. Scaffolding, in the context of zpd, is a term used for the process of support and guidance offered to help the student achieve at a different level. This concept has been extended to include the assessment of student performance and moves beyond static assessment of what is known to a more interactive model that considers learning potential (Gipps, 1994). The feedback and the use of progress maps in the portfolio process help to guide learning. Dialogue plays a critical role in this assessment, teaching and learning context. Helping the student to new developmental levels, guided learning and the role of dialogue are important considerations for the development of a portfolio of work.

Constructivist pedagogy

My argument is thus that portfolio use for assessment can support the learning process insofar as it aligns with constructivist learning theory which sees students as actively making sense of new knowledge and deciding how to integrate it with previously held concepts. It has been claimed that this emphasis in contemporary meaning-based pedagogies requires a rethinking of the 'instruction–curriculum–assessment triad' (Engel, 1994) so that curriculum design and teaching support assessment practices that promote intended learning. This requires an understanding of the principles that underpin constructivist conceptions of knowledge and pedagogical characteristics of constructivist teaching and learning.

Hendry (1996) has identified the following constructivist principles in relation to the conception of knowledge:

- knowledge exists only in the minds of people;
- the meanings or interpretations people give to things depend on their knowledge;
- knowledge is constructed from within in interrelation with the world;
- knowledge can never be certain;
- common knowledge derives from a common brain and body which are part of the same universe;
- knowledge is constructed through perception and action; and
- the construction of knowledge requires energy and time.

The implications for teachers are that they need to provide their students with opportunities to discuss, explain and evaluate their solutions in a problem-centred learning context. The teacher's role is to facilitate collaboration, group and pair work, and participation in class discussion. A teacher must ask questions to understand students' thinking and evaluate explicitly students' answers, correcting their misconceptions. Key skills for the teacher are listening and diagnosing the way students interpret activities to inform further action. Students develop views, acceptable for further learning, although such constructions can take time. The implication for teaching is that a non-threatening learning environment is vital. As a constructivist educator the teacher adopts the role of 'collaborator in the process of making sense of the world. Teachers guide construction by providing problems and collaborating with students during group or class discussion' (Hendry, 1996: 33). Trust is paramount.

The constructivist educator creates a learning environment that incorporates opportunities for an analysis of learning; teacher-facilitated learning; group and pair work; student–teacher dialogue about the student's learning; and consistently available support and collaboration. It is this pedagogical approach that is called for when portfolios are used for assessment and learning. The learning process for students in the development of a portfolio involves teacher attention to specific individual strengths and weaknesses without comparison to others. Specific feedback from the teacher that helps take learning forward, together with the student's own self-evaluations, help in the development of personal goals. They are motivated and inspired to establish high expectations. Collaboration with teachers encourages students to value the processes, products and themselves. This is because substantive conversation between student and teacher about learning is possible.

The constructivist theoretical underpinnings of such learning environments have been described by Ernest (cited in Murphy, 1997):

- knowledge as a whole is problematised, not just the learner's subjective knowledge, and includes mathematical knowledge and logic;
- methodological approaches are required to be much more circumspect and reflexive because there is no 'royal road' to truth or near truth;
- the focus of concern is not just the learner's cognitions, but the learner's beliefs, and conceptions of knowledge;
- the focus of concern with the teacher and in teacher education is not just with the teacher's knowledge of subject matter and diagnostic skills, but with the teacher's beliefs, conceptions and personal theories about subject matter, teaching and learning;
- although we can tentatively come to know the knowledge of others by interpreting their language and actions through our own conceptual constructs, the others have realities that are independent of ours . . . it is the realities of others along with our own realities that we strive to understand, but we can never take any of these realities as fixed;
- an awareness of the social construction of knowledge suggests a pedagogical emphasis on discussion, collaboration, negotiation and shared meanings (Ernest cited in Murphy, 1997: 3).

A constructivist paradigm for learning implies a certain pedagogy. Murphy (1997) has identified the characteristics that can serve as a checklist for teachers seeking to translate constuctivist learning theory into the reality of their classroom teaching and learning practices. Murphy warns that the checklist serves a limited purpose. Not all of the characteristics will be observed because much depends on the teacher and the group of students. Also not all learning environments are classroom-based, such as in the case of online and distance learning. However, these characteristics do provide an insight into how the theory might be translated into practice.

Pedagogical characteristics of constructivist classrooms

- Multiple perspectives and representations of concepts and content are presented and encouraged.
- Goals and objectives are derived by the student or in negotiation with the teacher or system.
- Teachers serve in the role of guides, monitors, coaches, tutors and facilitators.
- Activities, opportunities, tools and (learning) environments are provided to encourage metacognition, self-analysis, self-regulation, self-reflection and self-awareness.
- The student plays a central role in mediating and controlling learning.
- Learning situations, environments, skills, content and tasks are relevant, realistic and authentic, and represent complexities of the 'real world'.
- Primary sources of data are used in order to ensure authenticity and real-world complexity.
- Knowledge construction and not reproduction is emphasised.
- This construction takes place in individual contexts and through social negotiation, collaboration and experience.
- The learner's previous knowledge constructions, beliefs and attitudes are considered in the knowledge construction process.
- Problem solving, higher-order thinking skills and deep understanding are emphasised.
- Errors provide the opportunity for insight into students' previous knowledge constructions.
- Exploration is a favoured approach in order to encourage students to seek knowledge independently and to manage the pursuit of their goals.
- Learners are provided with the opportunity for apprenticeship learning in which there is an increasing complexity of tasks, skills and knowledge acquisition.
- Knowledge complexity is reflected in an emphasis on conceptual inter-relatedness and interdisciplinary learning.
- Collaborative and cooperative learning are favoured in order to expose the learner to alternative viewpoints.
- Scaffolding is facilitated to help students perform just beyond the limits of their ability.
- Assessment is authentic and interwoven with teaching (Murphy, 1997).

Conceptual framework

The conceptual framework that underpins this book is developed from a particular view of the nature of learning, learners and knowledge. These thoughts about learning and knowledge construction are made explicit to emphasise the implications for assessment of learning and how outcomes of the assessment process are interpreted and used. The importance of the relationship between the learner, learning and assessment is kept central to facilitate understanding and the development of pedagogic practice in the use of portfolios for learning and assessment purposes.

In accordance with the theories of learning presented by Dewey (1916), Vygotsky (1978) and Bruner (1990), learning in this book is seen as socially embedded: we learn by and with others. Social interaction is fundamental to learning for it is through interactive conversation that the development of an individual's ability to represent the world and to make meaning are facilitated.

Dewey (1916) warned that learning which focused on accumulation of information and reproduction for examination purposes was detrimental to educative development. He saw knowledge as fundamental to further learning and was critical of it being seen as an end in itself. His view was that students engaged in thinking when they had first-hand experience of grappling with the problem to find their own solutions. The teacher, he suggested, shared in the activity. He wrote:

> In such shared activity, the teacher is a learner, and the learner is, without knowing it a teacher – and upon the whole, the less consciousness there is, on either side, of either giving or receiving instruction, the better.
>
> (Ibid.: 188)

Dewey saw thinking as the method of an educative experience that corresponded to the essentials of reflection. These he outlined as follows:

- The pupil has a genuine situation of experience that is a continuous activity that holds his or her interest for its own sake.
- A genuine problem develops within the situation as a stimulus to thought.
- The student possesses the information and makes observations needed to deal with it.
- Suggested solutions occur and the student develops these in an orderly way.
- The student has the opportunity and occasion to test the ideas by application to make their meaning clear and to discover their validity (ibid.: 192).

Bruner (1990) too sees learners as constructors and generators of knowledge through social interaction and recursive thought. The implications for the curriculum and assessment are the need for dialogue and reflection to be incorporated into the learning process. Knowledge is conceived as an outcome of the activity, context and culture in which it is developed and used. Doll explains that it is through experience that we make reasoned choices but it is not experience only of doing; reflection on what we do is fundamental. It is 'experience that is analysed through the lenses of culture, language and personal bias' that knowledge is understood (Doll, 1993: 130). He explains further: 'knowledge is what we create – interactively, dialogically, conversationally – always within our culture and its language' (ibid.: 136).

The notion that knowledge is situated and develops in a dynamic and interactive way underpins the conceptual framework on which the design and development of a portfolio system of assessment has been conceptualised. This view of how we learn sees

> the activities of person and environment . . . as parts of a mutually constructed whole and a performance as the product of a history of relating, in which both person and environment change over the course of transaction.
>
> (Bredo, 1999: 33)

Writing, for instance, is described by Bredo as a 'mutual matter of composition' not a simple transfer of ideas from brain to paper. In the writing process there is drafting and redrafting incorporating changes and refinements to interpretation and expression. The emphasis is on the person acting with the environment, rather than on it, for the purposes of mutual modification to produce an integral accomplishment. From this perspective cognition and context are connected.

Situated cognition views knowledge as inseparable from what is learned or how it is learned, used and tested from the practices of the particular community of language users. Knowledge from this perspective is not separable from learning and cognition. It is viewed as a tool and is seen as the result of transaction or a process of inquiry. Like a tool, knowledge is best understood through its use, and by using that knowledge a change to the user's view of the world occurs, the belief system of the culture in which it is used is also adopted. Similarly, problem-solving is seen as inseparable from the activity in which consciousness arises and which facilitates successful conscious problem-solving (Bredo, 1999). Learning and cognition are fundamentally situated. The implication for teaching and assessment is that active learning in authentic social and physical contexts are more likely to result in providing useable, robust knowledge (Shepard, 1997).

A central tenet of a situated approach is that individual task performance is inseparable from change in the social relationships in which people participate. Bredo (1999) quotes Lave and Wegner's (1991) position:

> Learning is a process that takes place in a participation framework, not in an individual mind . . . it is mediated by the differences in perspective among the coparticipants. It is the community, or at least those participating in the learning context, who 'learn' under this definition. Learning is, as it were, distributed among the coparticipants, not a one-person act. While the apprentice may be the one transformed most dramatically by increased participation in a productive process it is the wider process that is the crucial

locus and precondition for this transformation . . . The larger community of practitioners reproduces itself through the formation of apprentices, yet it would presumably be transformed as well.

(Bredo, 1999: 39)

The work related to situated cognition is to some extent built on the research of Vygotsky (1978). He argued that higher order functions such as cognition develop in a social context. Individual development, he contended, could not be understood by only studying the individual, the particular social contexts in which that individual has developed also need to be examined. Similarly, interaction is dependent on language that is learnt in particular social contexts. The inter-relations between thought and language are crucial for the understanding of intellectual development and concept development. Language becomes essential in forming thought. Vygotsky (1962) indicated that the formation of new concepts occurs when the problem cannot otherwise be solved. He proposed that higher-order mental functions appear first on the social level between people and later on the individual level, inside the child.

A major implication for teaching is that interaction between teacher and learner is fundamental to learning and emphasises the importance of formative assessment. The teacher needs to assume a supportive rather than a directive role in the learning process. In this role the teacher ascertains the potential of the learner to proceed, so that the new challenges presented are achievable without being too insignificant or too challenging. The teacher needs to understand the student's existing ideas through encouraging student expression and presentation of them. The teacher needs to listen to the student, interpret what the student says and does and attempt to understand the student's conceptual constructions. In this way the learner's thinking is made explicit and the need for conceptual modification becomes apparent. The teacher is also able to monitor reconstruction and development. The student needs to be aware of the standards and how to achieve performance at these required levels.

The implication for assessment from this perspective is that an important function is to help identify a student's zone of proximal development and to explore progress within it. Formative assessment can help clarify the student's existing knowledge and reveal important aspects of understanding that can be developed. The teacher needs to find ways and contexts that challenge students' ideas, through experiences that are new and with which their current ideas cannot cope without modification. Teachers need to explore the student's responses to such challenge. Self-assessment and reflection become important assessment processes for making the students' thinking about their own learning explicit and accessible to the teacher. Students need to be able to determine if they are making progress and this requires the development of important strategies such as setting goals and self-evaluating at regular intervals to check progression.

Context for portfolio use

The context of the new millennium and the social realities of the new eclectic 'post' era – post-industrial, post-structural, post-modernist (Doll, 1993) – have placed new demands on assessment, pedagogy and curriculum development. These are times of rapid change that include radical intellectual, social and political shifts. Nations around the world are being affected by significant technological and social transformations, the consequences of which are difficult to predict.

The Organisation for Economic Co-operation and Development (OECD) in its launch of the Programme for International Student Assessment (PISA) (1999: 9) has adopted 'a dynamic model of lifelong learning in which new knowledge and skills necessary for successful adaptation to changing circumstances are continuously acquired over the life cycle'. The rationale is that schools cannot teach everything that the student will need to know in adult life. However, the acquisition of the prerequisites for successful learning in future life is possible. These prerequisites are cognitive and motivational and include: the ability to organise; to self-regulate one's learning; to be independent in learning as well as be able to learn in groups to achieve success. The implications are that students need to be aware of their own thinking processes, learning strategies and styles.

Information technology has been the driving force for change in a context of global economic networks. A blending of technologies such as mobile phones, fax machines, computers, telephones, televisions into a telecommunications industry is a reality and is a consequence of strategic alliances (Naisbitt, 1994). The subsequent revolution in information-sharing and the rapid development of technologies has accelerated the pace of change. What is valued today is speed and agility. Individuals are accessing more information at greater speed than ever before and communicating to others anywhere and at any time.

The emergence of the global economy has caused major restructuring of national economies and change to education systems in both developed and developing worlds. There exists 'the borderless global economy' (Lasch, 1996) with wealth being produced and distributed internationally through private networks (Blachford, 1997). Globalisation has resulted in the denationalisation of business enterprise, an increase in the global disparity between wealth and poverty (Lasch, 1996) and changes to the general nature of the labour market. Occupations continue to change with new ones created. Employees can expect to have multiple roles and to work on a number of projects, for different employers, in different locations and under different working conditions. Education is advocated as the way to prepare for the new forms and patterns of employment. Reich (1991) has argued that individuals need to enhance their skills and capacities and improve the linking of those skills and capacities to the world market. He has indicated that those who are skilled and insightful will earn more wealth, leaving the less skilled behind in a declining standard of living. Reich (1991) has identified three categories of employment: routine production service workers,[2] in-person service workers[3] and symbolic analysts.[4]

Social transformations and change in societal roles have made it difficult to identify *exactly* what society actually needs. Lasch (1996) has indicated that in

America it is the 'symbolic analysts' who are rising in the class structure while the other categories are declining in both wealth and status. He is critical of Reich's admiration for this group and his portrayal of them as the 'best and the brightest'. He emphasises that once a geographic concentration of these workers develops through 'networking', a market for the 'in-person server' category of worker emerges. This group then attends to the needs of the 'symbolic analysts'. The Silicon Valley and Hollywood are given as examples of these centres of technical and artistic enterprise that are segregating by income. Lasch (1996: 47) refers to Reich's account of how the global nature of business enterprise has produced 'a class of cosmopolitans who see themselves as world citizens, but without accepting . . . any of the obligations that citizenship in a polity normally implies'. He notes that this group of new elites is more willing to invest in their own privileged commu-nities in services such as private schools and private police rather than supporting public services.

Such changes in the labour market and societal roles suggest quality education for all and important implications for curriculum. Students need a high standard of general education and the ability to continue to learn whether they will be employers, managers or employees. Globalisation, rapid technological develop-ments and the exponential rate of growth in knowledge call for better curriculum, assessment and pedagogical decisions and practices. The increase in student retention rates, the multicultural nature of the population and occupational mobility are further reasons for improved practices. This combination of changes makes the notion of training specifically for a lifelong job anachronistic. The implications for education are numerous. *All* students need to acquire skills in self-management, self-regulation, continuing learning, self-evaluation and planning of future work.

In 1903 Dewey identified the skills students needed to take up their various roles in society, such as member of family, community, neighbourhood and worker. These skills included the capacity for independence of thought, automony in learning, self-direction, perseverance, habits of 'serviceableness' and responsibility for leadership. Ironically, educationalists and businesses are advocating similar skills today and civics or citizenship education is again on the educational agenda. Dewey's description of the ethical principles underlying education, which he saw as the same as those for society, emphasised the impossibility of 'educating the child for any fixed station in life'

> ethical responsibility of the school on the social side must be interpreted in the broadest and freest spirit, it is equivalent to that training of the child which will give him [sic] such possession of himself that he may take charge of himself; may not only adapt himself to the changes which are going on, but have power to shape and direct those changes.
>
> (1903: 12)

It is student agency that is lacking in current curriculum, pedagogy and assessment systems. Students today need to have the capacity to be 'self-actualising', to have a confidence with change, and the ability to manage hope for themselves, and others, for the future. They also need the opportunity to learn how to manage and take charge of change if, as they are finding themselves, they are in situations of rapid, radical changes of a global, economic, social and political nature.

The standard by which to judge the value of studies, according to Dewey, is the extent to which pupils' awareness of their social environment has increased and their ability to interpret their own powers in relation to possible social use has developed. Dewey (1903: 8) emphasised the importance of preparation for social life through engagement with social life. In considering the ethical principles from a psychological perspective he stated:

> conduct has to do, then with the question of agency, of how the individual operates; the social, with what the individual does and needs to do, considered from the standpoint of his membership in a whole which is larger than himself.

Dewey (1903: 10) continues:

> It is not the mere individual as individual who makes the final demand for moral action, who establishes the final end, or furnishes the final standards of worth. It is the constitution and development of the larger life into which he enters which settles these things. But when we come to the question of how the individual is to meet the moral demands, of how he is to realize the values within himself, the question is one which concerns the individual as an agent.

Dewey described social intelligence, social power and social interests as the 'moral trinity of the school' and he identified the resources for the realisation of these aims as the life of the school as a social institution itself, the methods of learning and doing work and the school curriculum. Social intelligence he defined as the capacity for observing and comprehending social situations and social power as taking charge and serving social interest and aims. He stressed the natural desire of children to 'give out, to do, and that means to serve' and believed that:

> the introduction of every method which appeals to the child's active powers, to his capacities in construction, production, and creation, marks an opportunity to shift the centre of ethical gravity from an absorption which is selfish to a service which is social.
>
> (Ibid.: 17)

Citizenship, values education, and skills such as creativity, critical thinking, initiative and flexibility are advocated for the demands of this century. Dewey stressed the importance of student agency and the implications for pedagogy. One hundred years on, important international trends, brought about by the telecommunications and technological revolution, have initiated changes that have important implications for assessment, pedagogy and the curriculum.

Curriculum for the twenty-first century

The accountability movement of the late 1980s, in countries such as Australia and England, led to policies of reregulation of curriculum and assessment resulting in technical solutions to the issue of educational reform, school development and improvement. These policies continue to significantly change the control over what is taught, how it is taught and how it is assessed to the detriment of teacher agency. In the 1990s, in England, for example, technicism and reductionism threatened curriculum policy and evaluation. These developments have been attacked by the educational profession and academics in defence of the intellectual rigour of their disciplines and practices. Educational researchers and academics (Gipps, 1994; Mabry, 1999; Shepard, 2000) have argued for educative forms of assessment, generative curriculum and pedagogic practices that honour teacher professionalism and student agency.

With information such as facts, codes, formulae and rules more readily accessible, what becomes a fundamental skill for survival in the information revolution is the 'creative and effective *use* of knowledge' (Reich, 1991). What the student can do with the knowledge is more important than whether the knowledge acquired is accurately recalled or 'matches a frame set by others' (Doll, 1993). Technicist and mechanistic approaches to the curriculum are retarding the development of skills and limiting essential experiences such as: experiential learning, accepting responsibility for continuing learning, collaborative learning, problem-identifying, analysing and solving, communicating abstract concepts and achieving consensus. Such learning is fundamental to the work of the 'symbolic analyst'. Transmission teaching and rote learning stifle curiosity, creativity and critique. Pedagogically curricula need to be multifaceted with a mixture of practices that are technological and innovative. Teachers' planning needs to be reflective and interactive. Processes of reflection, reorganisation and interaction are part of curriculum construction. Teachers need to theorise about their practice so that theory is grounded and developed from practice. Doll (1993) has referred to this as 'grounded knowing' as opposed to 'technical knowing.'

Doll offers a 'post-modernist, process-oriented vision' of curriculum and teaching that 'stretches and accommodates' to provide opportunities for students to gain skills, knowledge and attitudes that include reflective understanding, negotiation, interpretation, judgement, capacity to question, to be generative, to peer evaluate. The development of the self is important in this conceptualisation of a curriculum for this century. To be self-organising and to identify one's own needs will help heighten one's personal consciousness. Self-evaluation will continue to be important.

In his critique of current curriculum systems, Doll (1993) highlights the inadequacy:

- of the linear, sequential, easily measurable nature that ignores complexity, uncertainty and multifariousness;
- of closed systems that focus on product to the neglect of process; and

- of setting of goals, planning implementations and evaluating quantifiable results to the detriment of educative purpose, planning and evaluation that is open-ended and flexible.

He contrasts clearly the teaching of these curriculum systems. He advocates a post-modern curriculum of open-ended design to promote teaching that:

- encourages students to be active creators rather than passive receivers of knowledge;
- provides students with opportunities to exercise choice and leadership not ordering and following; and
- is interactive and uses communal conversation for dialogic learning not isolated and programmed learning approaches.

The theory of knowledge on which such a curriculum is conceived is interactive and dialogic. Knowledge creation, discovery and negotiation are emphasised rather than verification of meaning. It is a generative curriculum that facilitates the creative, interactive transformations between teacher and student, student and student.

Lawton (1998) has indicated that a curriculum for the twenty-first century requires a shift from content and objectives to skills and processes. Young (1999) describes a curriculum for the future as one that has a transformative concept of knowledge that emphasises empowerment of learners to act on the world. Other features of this curriculum include a focus on the creation of new knowledge, an emphasis on the interdependence of knowledge areas and on the relevance of school knowledge to everyday problems. These changing emphases and conceptions of curriculum suggest the need for corresponding changes to teachers' roles and responsibilities. Teachers need to shift from being implementers to creators and developers of curriculum.

This reconceptualisation of curriculum has important implications for the assessment of learning. A norm-referenced approach to assessment that is derived from a deficit model is no longer suitable. This is because the assessments of learning are made in terms of deviation from the norm or standard. Today, assessment of the quality of work generated is considered more important in a curriculum context that encourages feedback focused on learning purposes and that values critical, reflective, iterative processes for development and improvement. The notion of a portfolio of work, developed over time, incorporating critical reflection and self-evaluation of what has been achieved makes for a more compatible assessment system. Reflecting on the inclusions in the portfolio (assignments, written papers or tests), or what has been achieved, provides the opportunity for another level of analysis (internal analysis) of the extent to which intentions and purposes have been achieved.

Higher levels of thinking skills are required. Internationally, politicians and employers are making such demands. We need to empower students to learn. Assessment, pedagogic practice and curriculum need to be aligned so that active student engagement in learning is encouraged and opportunities exist for students to take greater responsibility for their learning. Student agency needs to be promoted. This requires educators, policy officers and political advisors to keep pace with the important developments in assessment and to understand the vital links between assessment and the teaching and learning cycle.

The use of a portfolio for assessment and learning purposes in education is a development that offers potential. Portfolio use in this context shifts the focus, in Dewey's words, from 'the target', the end, the product, to the broader educational aim of 'hitting the target'. The processes involved in this form of assessment encourage the learner to take responsibility for their own learning and to be reflective, a key tool for transformation and development. In the Report of the Steering Group of the National Record of Achievement Review (1997: 4–5) it is stated that:

> Many people are increasingly likely to live so-called 'portfolio lives', constantly needing to update their skills and knowledge in order to take advantage of opportunities as they arise. Their skills will need to be transferable.

And

> This changing world will thus place much greater emphasis on individuals taking responsibility for reflecting on what they have already experienced, setting future learning goals and preparing plans for how these will be achieved in order to improve their contribution and their employability.

This context has provided the impetus for this book. With societal demands for a more diverse range of skills and learning outcomes from students in the twenty-first century, teachers need to employ teaching and assessment approaches that will deliver. The use of a portfolio for assessment and learning may be one such approach.

Implications

Important implications for educators and policy-makers exist if alternative forms of assessment such as the portfolio are to be implemented with success. As has been discussed in chapter 4, too often the policy context can result in unintended consequences and unhelpful pressures on the development of assessment systems which prevent the realisation of the intended learning benefits from the use of portfolios. An understanding of the differences in assessment approaches and the different purposes of portfolio use as outlined in chapter 3 will help to coordinate assessment with teaching and learning.

Policy decisions need to be supportive and the prevailing conceptions of teaching and learning that underpin the assessment policy need to align with the intended purpose of the portfolio. Lessons can be learnt from the early experiences of portfolio use outlined in chapter 4. If the prevailing assessment context is one of measurement rather than of support for learning then the tensions and pressures will remain, preventing a climate conducive to developmental approaches to assessment, as embodied in the portfolio.

If portfolios are to be used for high-stakes purposes with associated content and performance standards then adequate educational resources and professional development to acquire competence with these changes need to occur before schools, teachers or students are described as failing to meet new standards. Change to assessment practices that incorporate the use of the portfolio will require corresponding changes to curriculum and pedagogy. It is not only teachers who need to learn about the pedagogical implications of the use of portfolios for assessment and learning; students also need specific teaching and support to develop the cognitive processes as outlined in chapter 2. Teachers need to reconceptualise their pedagogy to integrate portfolio processes into their routines and classroom teaching. When portfolios are introduced, time is needed for the evolution and development of practices, processes and procedures to be implemented in a systematic way. This will help to validate the methodology employed and enable research and evaluation into its effectiveness as an alternative to more reductionist forms of assessment.

The conception of the assessment of the portfolio and the assessment scheme adopted is a fundamental consideration in the implementation of the portfolio. The complications and problems that emerged from the detailed written standards of the assessment system as outlined in the case of the GNVQs in England and Wales need to be avoided. It is inappropriate to require exhaustive evidence to demonstrate the attainment of all outcomes specified, as in the case of the original GNVQs. It is more appropriate to sample key features to determine the 'best fit' according to a standards-referenced framework or a developmental continuum. It is crucial that professional judgement is valued and supported by cultivating shared communities of assessment practice. Time for assessors to develop an understanding of the standards should be considered and the development of communities of shared assessment practice facilitated.

This book has been an attempt to disseminate and extend the debate for assessment practices that honour teachers' professionalism and support student and teacher agency in the choice of means and processes of action for continued learning. If this book has 'roused to life' some discussion, debate or critique of current assessment practices then it has served its purpose.

Summary

- Portfolio use for assessment purposes parallels the shift from a quantitative tradition of assessment to a more qualitative approach.
- The reductionist nature and impact of external tests on learning, curriculum and pedagogy and the diminution of teacher and student agency are major reasons for dissatisfaction with conventional forms of assessment.
- Developments in constructivist theories of learning and educational assessment have supported the move towards authentic, alternative assessments, such as the portfolio.

- Portfolio use requires a constructivist pedagogy characterised by: opportunities to analyse learning; teacher facilitation of learning; group and pair work; student–teacher dialogue about the student's learning; available support and collaboration.
- Learning theories which describe learning as socially embedded – learning by and with others (Dewey, 1916; Vygotsky,1978; Bruner, 1990) – have underpinned the conceptualisation of portfolio use as presented in this book.
- All students need to acquire skills in self-management, self-regulation, continuing learning, self-evaluation and planning of future work because of the rapid, radical changes of a global, economic, social and political nature, implying necessary changes to assessment, pedagogy and the curriculum as described through the use of portfolios.

Notes

1 Using portfolios for a range of purposes

1   The term folio will be used in preference to the word portfolio in relation to the Scottish system and the Scottish Examination Board context.
2   Professionalism is used in this context to include theoretical knowledge, practical competence and commitment – see Pring, 1998.
3   Teachers' knowledge is detailed, contextually bound and extensive, and these qualities need to be acknowledged.

2 Key processes in portfolio development

1   Watkins et al. (1996) highlight higher-order processes as fundamental in defining effective learning. Watkins (2001) has distinguished between metacognition (thinking about thinking that involves awareness of thinking processes and 'executive control' of such processes) and metalearning (making sense of one's experience of learning which involves a wider range of issues including goals, feelings, social relations and context of learning).

3 Key concepts in portfolio assessment

1   Like those of the California Learning Assessment System (CLAS), organic portfolio assessment.

4 Problems and pitfalls

1   Part one GNVQ is a slimmer version of the GNVQ that has been designed primarily for fourteen- to sixteen-year-olds.

5 A case study

1   This was an art lesson involving charcoal drawing for class F2E.

7 Portfolios and changes in assessment

1   The first stage involves more capable others, assisting those who have limited understanding of the situation, task or goals, by direction or modelling. The child reproduces a response and gradually understands how the parts of an activity relate to one another and comes to understand the meaning of the performance. This is communicated through conversation during the performance of the task. When this understanding of

the overall performance is attained the child is ready to receive further guidance from questions, feedback and cognitive structuring. When the teacher offers selective assistance to a child or scaffolds learning, Tharp and Gallimore (1998) emphasise that the teacher is not simplifying the task. Rather they are maintaining the difficulty of the task while simplifying the child's role by offering graduated assistance. Teachers require a profound knowledge of the subject to be able to assist performance during this first stage. This is because the child may not conceptualise the learning goal in the same way as the teacher and during the assisted performance different goals and sub-goals emerge. That is, the child's goals will shift in response to the teacher's help. The teacher needs to be able to quickly reformulate the goals of the interaction to map the child's conception of the task goal onto the superordinate knowledge structures of the academic discipline that is being learnt. The desired outcome in this first stage of zpd is the emergence of self-regulation on the part of the child. When the child can begin to ask questions and communicate with the teacher to procure assistance, the teacher needs to provide assistance that is responsive to the child's current effort and understanding of the learning goal. The task of stage one is achieved when the student can assume responsibility for adapting the assistance, the transfer and can perform the task itself.

Stage two occurs when the student can perform the task without assistance from others but this does not mean that the performance is fully developed or automatic. Once the child can direct their behaviour with their own speech an important stage has been reached in the transition of the skill through zpd. What was assisted by another is now beginning to be directed by the self (1998: 37). Stage three occurs when the performance is developed and automatic. The task can be carried out smoothly and has been internalised and integrated. Assistance from the adult or the self is no longer required because performance has developed. Stage four occurs when some environmental change, individual stress, major upheaval or physical trauma causes the individual to no longer be able to carry out the task that they could once do automatically. Tharp and Gallimore maintain that making self-speech external is an effective way of restoring the capacity through recursion of the developmental process. The goal at this stage is to re-proceed through assisted performance to self-regulation and to exit the zpd into a new automatic performance of the task.

2   The routine production service workers include low and mid-level supervisors, managers, data entry and retrieval personnel and routine producers. The nature of the work is repetitive and tedious. The skills required vary from low- to high level technical or craft related and are occupation specific. They are attainable in primary/ secondary schools and/or by employment-related training and experience. The qualities of these workers are reliability, punctuality and capacity to follow directions. These workers are heavily regulated and supervised and remuneration is by hours of work performed or on the amount of work completed.

3   The in-person service workers include estate agents, teachers, secretaries, hospitality workers, drivers, cashiers, health care workers, solicitors, police and cleaners. These services are provided 'person-to-person' and therefore require good communication and interpersonal skills. Reliability, punctuality and pleasant demeanour are desirable qualities and remuneration is by time served or amount of work performed. Tertiary education, on-the-job training and experience are important.

4   The symbolic analysts include engineers, bankers, managers, researchers, executives, consultants, television producers, advertising agents, designers, artists and enter-tainers who are employed in public and private enterprises, usually full time and often on a limited contractual basis. The nature of the work is problem identifying, problem-solving and strategic brokering. Production is of high value-added goods and services. High levels of formal education are required for many occupations in this group. Data and information are the symbols or the raw material and the work

is 'brain-based' using analytic tools. 'State-of-the-art' skills are required including flexible and creative thinking, risk taking and entrepreneurship. Income is dependent on the quality, creativity and speed with which problems are solved, identified or brokered and may be highly variable over time. These workers are open to international competition and operate on a global scale (Blachford, 1997).

References

American Educational Research Association (AERA) (2000) 'AERA Position Statement Concerning High-Stakes Testing in PreK-12 Education', HYPERLINK (http://www.aera.net).

Archbald, D. A. and Newmann, F. M. (1988) *Beyond Standardized Testing: Assessing Authentic Academic Achievement in the Secondary Schools*, Reston, Virginia: National Association of Secondary School Principals.

Arter, J. A. and Spandel, V. (1992) 'Using Portfolios of Student Work in Instruction and Assessment', *Educational Measurement: Issues and Practice*, Spring, pp. 36–44.

Ashby, R. (1998) 'Career Entry Profile and Professional Portfolio, Post Graduate Certificate in Education Course 1998–1999', Institute of Education, University of London.

Assessment Reform Group (1999) *Assessment for Learning. Beyond the Black Box*, Cambridge: University of Cambridge School of Education.

Bailey, J. M. and Guskey, T. R. (2001) *Implementing Student-led Conferences*, Thousand Oaks, California: Corwin Press.

Baker, E. (1997) 'Policy and Technical Issues in Performance Assessment', paper presented at the International Conference on Advances in Assessment of Student Learning at the Chinese University of Hong Kong.

Barr, M. A., Craig, D. A., Fisette, D. and Syverson, M. A. (1999) *Assessing Literacy with the Learning Record: A Handbook for Teachers, Grades K-6*, Portsmouth: Heinemann.

Biggs, J. (ed.) (1996) *Testing: To Educate or To Select?*, Hong Kong: Hong Kong Educational Publishing Co.

Blachford. K. (1997) 'Labour Market Change as a Context for Teacher Education – The Case of Hong Kong', paper presented at the European Conference on Educational Research, Frankfurt, Germany.

Black, P. (1998) *Testing: Friend or Foe? Theory and Practice of Assessment and Testing*, London: Falmer Press.

Black, P. (1999) 'Assessment, Learning Theories and Testing Systems', in P. Murphy (ed.) *Learners, Learning and Assessment*, London: Paul Chapman Publishing, pp. 118–34.

Black P. and Wiliam, D. (1998) 'Assessment and Classroom Learning', *Assessment in Education: Principles, Policy and Practice*, 5, 1, pp. 7–74.

Brandt, R. (1992) 'On Performance Assessment: A Conversation with Grant Wiggins', *Educational Leadership*, 49, 8, pp. 35–7.

Bredo, E. (1999) 'Reconstructing Educational Psychology', in P. Murphy (ed.) *Learners, Learning and Assessment*, London: Paul Chapman Publishing, pp. 23–45.

Broadfoot, P. (1986) 'Profiling and the Affective Curriculum', *Journal of Curriculum Studies*, 19, 1, pp. 25–34.

Broadfoot, P. (1996) 'Liberating the Learner through Assessment', in G. Claxton, T. Atkinson, M. Osborn and M. Wallace (eds) *Liberating the Learner*, London: Routledge, pp. 32–44.

Broadfoot, P. (1998a) 'Records of Achievement and the Learning Society: A Tale of Two Discourses', *Assessment in Education: Principles, Policy and Practice*, 5, 3, pp. 447–77.

Broadfoot, P. (1998b) 'Records of Achievement and the Learning Society: The Challenge of Change', paper presented at the 24th Annual Conference of the International Association for Educational Assessment, Barbados, West Indies.

Broadfoot, P. and Pollard, A. (1997) *National Record of Achievement Review: Report of the Steering Group 1997*, Department for Education and Employment.

Brown, A. L. and Campione, J. C. (1990) 'Interactive Learning Environments and the Teaching of Science and Maths', in M. Gardner, J. Greens, F. Reif, A. Schoenfeld, A. di Sessa and E. Stage (eds) *Toward a Scientific Practice of Science Education*, Hillsdale, New Jersey: Erlbaum, pp. 111–139.

Bruner, J. S. (1986) *Actual Minds, Possible Worlds*, Cambridge, Massachusetts: Harvard University Press.

Bruner, J. S. (1990) *Acts of Meaning*, Cambridge, Massachusetts: Harvard University Press.

Burke, P. and Rainbow, B. (1998) 'How to Compile a Portfolio', *Times Higher Educational Supplement*, 30 October, pp. 30–1.

Callahan, S. (1997) 'Tests Worth Taking? Using Portfolios for Accountability in Kentucky', *Reseach in the Teaching of English*, 31, 3, pp. 295–336.

Claxton, G. (1999) *Wise-Up: The Challenge of Lifelong Learning*, London: Bloomsbury.

Cole, D. J., Ryan, C. W., Kick, F. and Mathies, B. K. (2000) *Portfolios across the Curriculum and Beyond*, Thousand Oaks, California: Sage Publications.

Confey, J. (1990) 'What Constructivism Implies for Teaching', in R. B. Davis, C. A. Maher and N. Noddings (eds) *Constructivist Views on the Teaching and Learning of Mathematics*, *Journal for Research in Mathematics Education*, Monograph 4, Virginia: The National Council of Teachers of Mathematics, pp. 107–22.

Cormack, P., Johnson, B., Peters, J., and Williams, D. (eds) (1998) *Authentic Assessment: A Report on Classroom Research and Practice in the Middle Years*, Deakin, ACT: Australian Curriculum Studies Association.

Cresswell, M. (1996) 'What Are Examination Standards? The Role of Values in Large Scale Assessment', paper presented at the 22nd Annual International Association for Educational Assessment, Beijing, China.

Crockett, T. (1998) *The Portfolio Journey: A Creative Guide to Keeping Student-Managed Portfolios in the Classroom*, Colorado: Teacher Ideas Press.

Crooks, T. J. (1988) 'The Impact of Classroom Evaluation Practices on Pupils', *Review of Educational Research*, 58, pp. 438–81.

Cuban, L. (1998) 'A Post-Tenure Review Portfolio: A Collaborative Venture', in N. Lyons (ed.) *With Portfolio in Hand: Validating the New Teacher Professionalism*, New York: Teachers College Press, pp. 172–185

Darling-Hammond, L. (1991) 'The Implications of Testing Policy for Quality and Equality', *Phi Delta Kappan*, 73, 3, pp. 220–5.

Darling-Hammond, L., Ancess, J. and Falk, B. (1995) *Authentic Assessment in Action Studies of Schools and Students at Work*, New York: Teachers College Press.

Davidson, J. E., Deuser, R. and Sternberg, R. J. (1994) 'The Role of Metacognition in Problem Solving', in J. Metcalfe and A. P. Shimamura (eds) *Metacognition Knowing about Knowing*, Massachusetts: Massachusetts Institute of Technology, pp. 207–26.

Davis, C. L. and Honan, E. (1998) 'Reflections on the Use of Teams to Support the

Portfolio Process', in N. Lyons (ed.) *With Portfolio in Hand: Validating the New Teacher Professionalism*, New York: Teachers College Press, pp. 90–102.

Davydov, V. V. (1995) 'The Influence of L.S. Vygotsky on Education Theory, Research and Practice', *Educational Researcher*, 24, 3, pp. 12–21.

Department for Education and Employment (1997) *National Record of Achievement Review: Report of the Steering Group*, London: DFEE.

Department of Education and Science (1998) *Task Group on Assessment and Testing – National Curriculum: A Report*, London: Department of Education and Science.

Dewey, J. (1903) 'Ethical Principles Underlying Education', reprinted from *The Third Yearbook of the National Herbart Society*, Chicago: University of Chicago Press.

Dewey, J. (1916) *Democracy and Education: An introduction to the Philosophy of Education*, New York: Macmillan.

Dewey, J. (1933) *How We Think: A Restatement of the Relation of the Reflective Thinking to the Education Process*, London: D. C. Heath.

Doll, William, E., Jr (1993) *A Post-Modern Perspective on Curriculum*, New York: Teachers College Press.

Dwyer, C. A. (1994) 'Development of the Knowledge Base for the Praxis III: Classroom Performance Assessments Assessment Criteria', Princeton, New Jersey: Educational Testing Service.

Dwyer, C. A. (1998) 'Assessment and Classroom Learning: Theory and Practice', *Assessment in Education*, 5, 1, pp. 131–7.

Education Commission (1992) *Report No. 5 The Teaching Profession*, Hong Kong: Government Printer.

Education Commission (1996) *Report No. 7 Quality School Education*, Hong Kong: Government Printer.

Education Department of Western Australia (1996) *Spelling Developmental Continuum*, Melbourne: Addison Wesley Longman Australia.

Education Department of Western Australia (1997a) *Preparing a Teaching Portfolio: Guidelines for Applicants*, Perth: Education Department of Western Australia.

Education Department of Western Australia (1997b) *Student Outcome Statements 1997 Sample Book*, Perth: Education Department of Western Australia.

Education Department of Western Australia (1997c) *Continuum of the Use of Text Forms, Levels and Indicators of Student Behaviours*, Perth: Education Department of Western Australia.

Engel, B. S. (1994) 'Portfolio Assessment and the New Paradigm: New Instruments and New Places', *The Educational Forum*, 49, pp. 22–7.

Eraut, M., Steadman, S., Trill, J. and Porkes, J. (1996) 'The Assessment of NVQs', Research Report 4, University of Sussex Institute of Education.

Flutter, Julia., Kershner, Ruth and Rudduck, Jean (1999) 'Thinking about Learning, Talking about Learning'. A report of the Effective Learning Project, Cambridge: Homerton College.

Forster, M. and Masters, G. (1996) *Portfolios*, Victoria: Australian Council for Educational Research.

Francis, H. (1994) *Teachers Listening to Learners' Voices*, London: The British Psychological Society.

Freidus, H. (1998) 'Mentoring Portfolio Development', in N. Lyons (ed.) *With Portfolio in Hand: Validating the New Teacher Professionalism*, New York: Teachers College Press, pp. 41–50.

Gardner, H. (1983) *Frames of Mind*, New York: Basic Books.

Gardner, H. (1992) 'Assessment in Context: The Alternative to Standardized Testing', in B. R. Gifford and M. C. O'Connor (eds) *Changing Assessments: Alternative Views of Aptitude, Achievement and Instructions*, London: Kluwer Academic Publishers, pp. 77–119.

Gardner, I. and Edwards, J. (1998) *Scholastic Portfolio Assessment Maths Assessment: Key Stage 2 Scottish Levels C–E*, Warwickshire: Scholastic Limited.

Gifford, B. R. and O'Connor, M. C. (eds) (1994) *Changing Assessments: Alternative Views of Aptitude, Achievement and Instructions*, London: Kluwer Academic Publishers.

Gipps, C. (1994) *Beyond Testing: Towards A Theory of Educational Assessment*, London: Falmer Press.

Gipps, C. (1997) 'Achievement, Equity and Pedagogy: A view from England', paper presented at the 23rd Annual Conference of the International Association for Educational Assessment, Dunbau, South Africa.

Gipps, C. (1998a) 'Student Assessment and Learning for a Changing Society', *Prospects*, 28, pp. 31–44.

Gipps, C. (1998b) 'Socio-Cultural Perspectives on Assessment', paper presented at the 24th Annual Conference of the International Association for Educational Assessment, Barbados, West Indies.

Glaser, R. (1963) 'Instructional Technology and the Measurement of Learning Outcomes: Some Questions', *American Psychologist*, 18, pp. 519–21.

Glaser, R. (1990) 'Toward New Models for Assessment', *International Journal of Educational Research*, 14, 5, pp. 475–83.

Grant, G. E. and Huebner, T. A. (1998) 'The Portfolio Question: The Power of Self-Directed Inquiry,' in N. Lyons (ed.) *With Portfolio in Hand: Validating the New Teacher Professionalism*, New York: Teachers College Press, pp. 156–71.

Griffin, P. (1998a) 'Outcomes and Profiles: Changes in Teachers' Assessment Practices', *Curriculum Perspectives*, 18, 1, pp. 9–19.

Griffin, P. (1998b) 'Profiles and Reporting in a Developmental Assessment Framework', *Incorporated Association of Registered Teachers of Victoria (IARTV)*, 75, pp. 3–20.

Guba, E. G. and Lincoln, Y. S. (1989) *Fourth Generation Evaluation*, New York: Sage.

Guttenplan, D. D. (2001) 'Testing our Children to Destruction', *Guardian G2*, 4 July 2001, p. 5.

Hacker, Douglas J. (1998) 'Definitions and Empirical Foundations', in D. J. Hacker, J. Dunlosky and A. C. Graesser (eds) *Metacognition in Educational Theory and Practice*, New Jersey: Lawrence Erlbaum Associates Publishers, pp. 1–23.

Hackett, G. (2001) 'Architect of AS-level Doubts Own Exam', *The Sunday Times*, 10 June 2001, p. 5.

Harlen, W. and James, M. (1997) 'Assessment and Learning: Differences and Relationships between Formative and Summative Assessment', *Assessment in Education: Principles, Policy and Practice*, 4, 3, pp. 365–79.

Harnisch, D. L. and Mabry, L. (1993) 'Issues in the Development and Evaluation of Alternative Assessments', *Journal of Curriculum Studies*, 25, 2, pp. 179–87.

Hattie, J. and Jaeger, R. (1998) 'Assessment and Classroom Learning: A Deductive Approach', *Assessment in Education: Principles, Policy and Practice*, 5, 1, pp. 112–20.

Heller, J. I., Sheingold, K. and Myford, C. M. (1998) 'Reasoning about Evidence in Portfolios: Cognitive Foundations for Valid and Reliable Assessment', *Educational Assessment*, 5, pp. 5–40.

Hendry, G. D. (1996) 'Constructivism and Educational Practice', *Australian Journal of Education*, 40, 1, pp. 19–45.

Henry, J. (2001) 'Time Has Come to Trust the Teachers', *Times Educational Supplement*, 29 June 2001, p. 2

Herman, J. L., Gearhart, M. and Baker, E. L. (1993) 'Assessing Writing Portfolios: Issues in the Validity and Meaning of Scores', *Educational Assessment*, 1, 3, pp. 201–24.

Hootstein, E. W. (1999) 'Implications of Using Portfolios with Preservice Social Studies Teachers', paper presented at the annual conference of the American Educational Research Association, Montreal, Canada.

Jarvinen, A. and Kohonen, V. (1995) 'Promoting Professional Development in Higher Education through Portfolio Assessment', *Assessment and Evaluation in Higher Education*, 20, 1, pp. 25–36.

Kimball, W. H. and Hanley, S. (1998) 'Anatomy of a Portfolio Assessment System: Using Multiple Sources of Evidence for Credentialing and Professional Development', in N. Lyons (ed.) *With Portfolio in Hand: Validating the New Teacher Professionalism*, New York: Teachers College Press, pp. 189–201.

King, B. (1991) 'Thinking about Linking Portfolios with Assessment Centre Exercises: Examples from the Teacher Assessment Project', *Teacher Education Quarterly*, 18, 3, pp. 31–48.

Koretz, D. (1998) 'Large-Scale Portfolio Assessments in the US: Evidence Pertaining to the Quality of Measurement', *Assessment in Education: Principles, Policies and Practice*, 5, 3, pp. 309–34.

Lasch, C. (1996) *The Revolt of the Elites and the Betrayal of Democracy*, New York. W.W. Norton.

Lawton, D. (1998) 'Values and Education: A Curriculum for the 21st Century', lecture, Institute of Education, University of London.

Lieberman, A. (1991) 'Accountability as a Reform Strategy', *Phi Delta Kappan*, 73, 3, pp. 219–20.

Lofty, J. S. (1993) 'Can Britain's National Curriculum Show America the Way?' *Educational Leadership*, 50, 5, pp. 52–5.

Looney, A. (2000) 'Between Hope and Despair: Towards a New Symbiosis of Curriculum and Assessment', Portfolio Assignment for Doctor in Education Programme, London, Institute of Education, University of London.

Lyons, N. (ed.) (1998a) *With Portfolio in Hand: Validating the New Teacher Professionalism*, New York: Teachers College Press.

Lyons, N. (1998b) 'Portfolio Possibilities: Validating a New Teacher Professionalism', in N. Lyons (ed.) *With Portfolio in Hand: Validating the New Teacher Professionalism*, New York: Teachers College Press, pp. 11–22.

Lyons, N. (1998c) 'Constructing Narratives for Understanding: Using Portfolio Interviews to Scaffold Teacher Reflection', in N. Lyons (ed.) *With Portfolio in Hand: Validating the New Teacher Professionalism*, New York: Teachers College Press, pp. 103–119

Mabry, L. (1999) *Portfolios Plus: A Critical Guide to Alternative Assessment*, Thousand Oaks: Corwin Press.

McClure, R. M. and Walters, J. (1992) 'Alternative Forms of Assessment', paper presented at the American Educational Research Association Conference, San Francisco.

McDowell, L. and Sambell, K. (1999) 'Fitness for Purpose in the Assessment of Learning: Students as Stakeholders', *Quality in Higher Education*, 5, 2, pp. 107–22.

Masters, G. (1997) 'Developmental Assessment: What, Why, How', paper presented at the International Conference on Advances in Assessment of Student Learning at the Chinese University of Hong Kong.

Maxwell, G. (1993) 'Criteria and Standards Based Assessment in Applied Statistical Mathematics', in J. Izard and M. Stephens (eds) *Reshaping Assessment Practices: Assessment in the Mathematical Sciences Under Challenge*, Proceedings of the First International Conference on Assessment in the Mathematical Sciences, Geelong, October, 1992, Victoria: Australian Council for Educational Research.

Maxwell, G. S. and Cumming, J. J. (1998) 'Reforming the Culture of Assessment: Changes in Teachers' Assessment Beliefs And Practices under a School-Based Assessment Regime', paper presented at the 24th Annual Conference of the International Association for Educational Assessment, Barbados, West Indies.

Messick, S. (1989) 'Validity', in R. Linn (ed.) *Educational Measurement* (3rd edn), American Council on Education, Washington: Macmillan.

Messick, S. (1994) 'The Interplay of Evidence and Consequences in the Validation of Performance Assessments', *Educational Researcher*, 23, 2, pp. 13–23.

Messick, S. (1995) 'Validity of Psychological Assessment: Validation of Inferences from Persons' Responses and Performances as Scientific Enquiry into Score Meaning', *American Psychologist*, 50, pp. 741–9.

Metcalfe, J. and Shimamura, A. P. (eds) (1994) *Metacognition Knowing about Knowing*, Massachusetts: Massachusetts Institute of Technology.

Morris, P. (1985) Teachers' Perceptions of the Barriers to the Implementation Of A Pedagogic Innovation: A South East Asian Case Study, *International Review of Education*, 3, pp. 3–18.

Moss, P. (1992) 'Shifting Conceptions of Validity in Educational Measurement: Implications for Performance Assessment', *Review of Educational Research*, 62, pp. 229 58.

Moss, P. (1994) 'Can There be Validity without Reliability?', *Educational Researcher*, 23, pp. 5–12.

Moss, P. (1998) 'Rethinking Validity for the Assessment of Teaching', in N. Lyons (ed) *With Portfolio in Hand: Validating the New Teacher Professionalism*, New York: Teachers College Press.

Munby, S. with Philips, P. and Collinson, R. (1989) *Assessing and Recording Achievement*, Oxford: Blackwell Education.

Murphy, E. (1997) *Constructivist Epistemology*, http://www.stemnet.nf.ca/~elmurphy/emurphy/cle2.html.

Naisbitt, J. (1994) *Global Paradox, The Bigger the World Economy, the More Powerful its Smallest Players*, London: Nicholas Brealey Publishing.

National Council for Vocational Qualifications (1995) 'Unit 1 Business Organisations and Employment (Intermediate)', London: National Council for Vocational Qualifications.

National Record of Achievement Review (1997) *Report of the Steering Group*, Cambertown.

Nelson, T. O. and Narens, L. (1994) 'Why Investigate Metacognition?' in J. Metcalfe and A. P. Shimamura (eds) *Metacognition Knowing about Knowing*, Massachusetts: Massachusetts Institute of Technology, pp. 1–25.

Newmann, F. (1991) 'Linking Restructuring to Authentic Student Achievement', *Phi Delta Kappan*, 72, 6, pp. 458–63.

Nitko, A. J. (1998) 'Seven Conceptual Frameworks to Accommodate the Validation of Rapidly Changing Requirements for Testing and Evaluation', Invited address presented at the 24th Conference of the International Association for Educational Assessment, Barbados.

Nuttall, D. (1987) 'The Validity of Assessments', *European Journal of Psychology of Education*, II, pp. 109–18.

Organisation for Economic Co-operation and Development (1999) *Measuring Student Knowledge and Skills: A New Framework for Assessment*, Paris: OECD.

Owens, G. and Soule, L. (1971) 'The Individual Profile', *Forum*, 13, Spring.

Paris, S. G. and Winograd, P. (1990) 'How Metacognition Can Promote Academic Learning and Instruction', in B. Fly Jones and L. Idol (eds) *Dimensions of Thinking and Cognitive Instruction*, New Jersey: Lawrence Erlbaum, pp. 15–51.

Paul, R. W. (1990) 'Critical and Reflective Thinking: A Philosophical Perspective', in B. Fly Jones and L. Idol (eds) *Thinking and Cognitive Instruction*, New Jersey: Lawrence Erlbaum.

Perrone, V. (ed.) (1991) *Expanding Student Assessment*, Virginia: Association for Supervision and Curriculum Development.

Pietroni, R. and Millard, L. (1997) 'Portfolio-Based Learning', in D. Pendleton and J. Hasler (eds) *Professional Development in General Practice*, Oxford: Oxford University Press, pp. 81–93.

Pring, R. (1998) 'Universities and Teacher Education', paper presented at the Annual Conference of the Standing Conference on Studies in Education, London.

Reich, R. B. (1991) *The Work of Nations Preparing Ourselves for Twenty First Century Capitalism*, New York: Vintage Books.

Resnick, L. B. and Resnick, D. P. (1992) 'Assessing the Thinking Curriculum: New Tools for Educational Reform', in B. R. Gifford and M. C. O'Connor (eds) *Changing Assessments: Alternative Views of Aptitude, Achievement and Instructions*, London: Kluwer Academic Publishers, pp. 37–75.

Richert, A. E. (1990) 'Teaching Teachers to Reflect: A Consideration of Programme Structure', *Journal of Curriculum Studies*, 22, 6, pp. 509–27.

Rieber, R. W. and Carton, A. S. (eds) (1987) *The Collected Works of L. S. Vygotsky, Volume 1, Problems of General Psychology*, London: Plenum Press.

Roe, E. (1987) 'How to Compile a Teaching Portfolio: A FAUSA Guide', Melbourne. FAUSA.

Rogoff, B. (1999) 'Cognitive Development through Social Interaction: Vygotsky and Piaget', in P. Murphy (ed.) *Learners, Learning and Assessment*, London: Paul Chapman Publishing, pp. 69–82.

Rosenshine, B. and Meister, C. (1994) 'Reciprocal Teaching: A View of the Research', *Review of Educational Research*, 64, 4, pp. 479–530.

Sacks, P. (1999) *Standardized Minds: The High Price of America's Testing Culture and What We Can Do to Change It*, Cambridge, Massachusetts: Perseus Books.

Sadler, R. (1985) 'The Origins and Functions of Evaluative Criteria', *Educational Theory*, 35, 3, pp. 285–97.

Sadler, R. (1989) 'Formative Assessment and the Design of Instructional Systems', *Instructional Science*, 18, 2, pp. 119–44.

Sadler, R. (1998) 'Formative Assessment: Revisiting the Territory', *Assessment in Education: Principles, Policy and Practice*, 5, pp. 77–84.

Salinger, T. (1998) 'Consequential Validity of an Early Literacy Portfolio: The "Backwash" of Reform', in C. Harrison and T. Salinger (eds) *Assessing Reading 1: Theory and Practice*, London: Routledge, pp. 182–203.

Schön, D. (1983) *The Reflective Practitioner: How Professionals Think in Action*, New York: Basic Books.

Schön, D. (1987) *Educating the Reflective Practitioner: Towards A New Design For Teaching and Learning in the Professions*, San Francisco: Jossey-Bass.

Schön, D. (1991) *The Reflective Turn: Case Studies In and On Educational Practice*, New York: Teachers College Press.

Scottish Examination Board (1991) *Scottish Certificate of Education, English (Revised) on the Higher Grade, Guidance for Teachers on Assessment, Part 1 The Personal Studies Folio*, Midlothian: Scottish Examination Board.

Scottish Examination Board (1992) *Certificate of Sixth Year Studies English, Guidance for Teachers on the Creative Writing Folio, Part 1: The Reflective Essay*, Midlothian: Scottish Examination Board.

Scottish Examination Board (1994a) *Higher Grade English Personal Studies Folio Guidance for Candidates*, Midlothian: Scottish Examination Board.

Scottish Examination Board (1994b) *Higher Grade English Personal Studies Folio Guidance for Teachers*, Midlothian: Scottish Examination Board.

Scottish Examination Board (1996) *Summary of Arrangements for Secondary Grade and Higher Grade English*, Midlothian: Scottish Examination Board.

Shepard, L. A. (1992) 'What Policy Makers Who Mandate Tests Should Know about the New Psychology of Intellectual Ability and Learning', in B. R. Gifford and M. C. O'Connor (eds) *Changing Assessments: Alternative Views of Aptitude, Achievement and Instructions*, London: Kluwer Academic Publishers. pp. 301–28.

Shepard, L. (1997) 'Measuring Achievement: What Does it Mean to Test for Robust Understanding?', Princeton, New Jersey: Policy Information Centre, Educational Testing Service.

Shepard, L. (2000) 'The Role of Assessment in a Learning Culture', Presidential Address presented at the annual meeting of the American Educational Research Association, New Orleans, 26 April.

Shulman, L. (1992) 'Portfolios in Teacher Education: A Component of Reflective Teacher Education', paper presented at the annual meeting of the American Educational Research Association, San Francisco.

Shulman, L. (1998) 'Teacher Portfolios: A Theoretical Activity', in N. Lyons (ed.) *With Portfolio in Hand: Validating the New Teacher Professionalism*, New York: Teachers College Press, pp. 23–37.

Simons, H. (1987) *Getting to Know Schools in a Democracy: The Politics and Process of Evaluation*, London: Falmer Press.

Smith, K. (1994) 'Evaluation-Assessment-Testing What? How? Who?', paper presented at the 28th International IATEFL Conference, Brighton.

Snadden, D. and Thomas, M. (1998) 'The Use of Portfolio Learning in Medical Education', *Medical Teacher*, 20, 3, pp. 192–99.

Snyder, J., Lippincott, A. and Bower, D. (1998) 'Portfolios in Teacher Education: Technical or Transformational?', in N. Lyons, (ed.) *With Portfolio in Hand: Validating the New Teacher Professionalism*, New York: Teachers College Press, pp. 123–42.

Stake, R. (1979) 'Counterpoint: Should Educational Evaluation Be More Objective or More Subjective?', *Educational Evaluation and Policy Analysis*, 1, 1, pp. 46–7.

Stecher, B. (1998) 'The Local Benefits and Burdens of Large-Scale Portfolio Assessment', *Assessment in Education: Principles, Policies and Practice*, 5, 3, pp. 335–51.

Stenhouse, L. (1975) *An Introduction to Curriculum Research and Development*, London: Heinemann.

Stiggins, R. (1992) 'Two Disciplines or Educational Assessment', paper presented at ECS Assessment Conference, June, Boulder, Colorado.

Stobart, G. (2001) 'The Short, but Eventful, History of GNVQ Assessment', internal paper, Insitute of Education, University of London.

Stone, B. (1998) 'Reflection in Teaching: Can it Be Developmental? A Portfolio Perspective', *Teacher Education Quarterly*, 25, 1, pp. 105–14.

Suarez, T. M. and Gottovi, N. C. (1992) 'The Impact of High Stakes Assessments on our Schools', *NASSP Bulletin*, September 1992, pp. 82–8.

Supovitz, J. A., Mac Gowan III, A. and Slattery, J. (1997) 'Assessing Agreement: An Examination of the Interrater Reliability of Portfolio Assessment in Rochester New York', *Educational Assessment*, 4, 3, pp. 237–59.

Targett, S. (1998) 'Future of the A-Level 'Too Narrow, Too Specialised, Too Elitist', in *Financial Times*, 3–4 October, p. vii.

Tharp, R. G. and Gallimore, R. (1988) *Rousing Minds to Life: Teaching, Learning and Schooling in Social Context*, Cambridge: Cambridge University Press.

Torrance, H. (1997) 'Assessment, Accountability and Standards: Using Assessment to Control the Reform of Schooling', in A. H. Halsey, H. Lauder, P. Brown and A. S. Wells (eds) *Education Culture, Economy, and Society*, Oxford: Oxford University Press.

Torrance, H. (2000) 'Postmodernism and Educational Assessment', in A. Filer (ed.) *Assessment: Social Practice and Social Product*, London: RoutledgeFalmer, pp. 173–88.

Torrance, H. and Pryor, J. (1998) *Investigating Formative Assessment: Teaching, Learning and Assessment in the Classroom*, Buckingham: Open University Press.

Vavrus, L. G. and Collins, A. (1991) 'Portfolio Documentation and Assessment Centre Exercises: A Marriage Made for Teacher Assessment', *Teacher Education Quarterly*, 18, 3, pp. 13–29.

Vygotsky, L. S. (1962) *Thought and Language*, Cambridge, Massachusetts: Massachusetts Institute of Technology Press.

Vygotsky, L. S. (1978) *Mind in Society*, Cambridge, Massachusetts: Harvard University Press.

Watkins, C. (2001) *Learning about Learning Enhances Performance*, London: Institute of Education School Improvement Network (Research Matters series no. 13).

Watkins, C., Carnell, E., Lodge, C. and Whalley, C. (1996) *Effective Learning*, London: Institute of Education School Improvement Network (Research Matters series no. 5).

Wiggins, G. (1989) 'A True Test: Toward More Authentic And Equitable Assessment', *Phi Delta Kappan*, 70, 9, pp. 703–13.

Wiggins, G. (1991) 'Standards, Not Standardization: Evoking Quality Student Work', *Educational Leadership*, 48, 5, pp. 18–25.

Wildy, H. and Wallace, J. (1997) 'Portfolios for Students and Teachers: Possibilities and Pointers for Practice', *Practising Administrator*, 3, pp. 10–15.

Wiliam, D. and Black, P. (1996) 'Meanings and Consequences: A Basis for Distinguishing Formative and Summative Functions of Assessment', *British Educational Research Journal*, 22, pp. 537–48.

Williams, K. (1992) *Assessment: A Discussion Paper*, Ireland: Cumann na Meanmhuinteoiri, Eire Association of Secondary Teachers.

Wolf, A. (1993) 'Assessment Issues and Problems in a Criterion Based System', Occasional Paper no. 2, London: Further Education Unit.

Wolf, A. (1998) 'Portfolio Assessment as National Policy: The National Council for Vocational Qualifications and its Quest for a Pedagogical Revolution', *Assessment in Education: Principles, Policy and Practice*, 5, 3, pp. 413–45.

Wolf, D. P. (1989) 'Portfolio Assessment: Sampling Student Work'. *Educational Leadership*, 46, 7, pp. 4–10.

Wolf, K. (1991) 'The School Teacher's Portfolio: Issues in Design, Implementation and Evaluation', *Phi Delta Kappan*, 73, 2, pp. 129–36.

Wolf, K., Whinery, B. and Hagerty, P. (1995) 'Teaching Portolios and Portfolio Conversations for Teacher Educators and Teachers', *Action in Teacher Education*, 17, 1, pp. 30–9.

Wyatt III, R. L. and Looper, S. (1999) *So You Have to Have a Portfolio: A Teacher's Guide to Preparation and Presentation*, Thousand Oaks: Corwin Press.

Young, M. (1999) 'The Curriculum of the Future', *British Educational Research Journal*, 25, 4, pp. 463–77.

Zessoules, R. and Gardner, H. (1991) 'Authentic Assessment: Beyond the Buzzword and into the Classroom', in V. Perrone (ed.) *Expanding Student Assessment*, Alexandria, Virginia: Association for Supervision and Curriculum Development, pp. 47–71.

Index